ISLAND HOPPING

AMANDA LINDROTH DESIGN

ISLAND HOPPING

AMANDA LINDROTH DESIGN

AMANDA LINDROTH
PHOTOGRAPHY BY TRIA GIOVAN
ILLUSTRATIONS BY ALDOUS BERTRAM

VENDOME
NEW YORK

CONTENTS

INTRODUCTION ~ 7

HOPE HILL ~ 15

BAYVIEW ~ 31

MINI SALT BOX ~ 49

WINDWHISTLE ~ 59

WATER MARTINS ~ 73

THE DUNMORE ~ 87

ANGLER'S COTTAGE ~ 95

HAVEN HILL ~ 105

MOON STONE FARM ~ 115

SPURLING POINT ~ 121

LA PALOMA ~ 131

BIENESTAR ~ 139

PALMETTO HOUSE ~ 147

OLD FORT BAY CLUB ~ 153

SCHOONER CABANA ~ 163

LILY PAD ~ 173

COMPASS POINT ~ 183

CHICCHARNEY ~ 195

TREE HOUSE ~ 207

MAHOGANY BAY ~ 217

CA'LIZA ~ 223

L'ORANGERIE ~ 235

POINT OF VIEW ~ 247

GOOMBAY ~ 257

WORTH AVENUE ~ 271

ISLAND HOPPING DAYS ~ 285

SOURCES ~ 300

ACKNOWLEDGMENTS ~ 302

INTRODUCTION

The little town of Palm Beach sits at the far north end of an eighteen-mile-long barrier island, with the beautiful strip called Manalapan at its southern tip. It is not a remote, isolated island, but it is the first island I fell in love with.

My parents were Philadelphians who spent a very long honeymoon in South Florida. My chic, cosmopolitan mother claimed that my father trapped her in Florida after they were married in 1960. Many years later, she told me that as a young newlywed she was not rich enough for a grand house in Palm Beach but refused to live in a Florida "ranch" house. So, to make the best of her Florida life, she hired a Danish modern architect for our family houses and started an important historical society, followed by a state preservation agency for architecture.

My mother's eye, I always say, helped to form my eye. As a very young Floridian in the 1970s I watched the burgeoning growth of the state as a place for full-time residents. It was in stark contrast to the previous Florida booms, which had largely been about winter-only residents and snow-fleeing tourists.

Our little primary school, Gulf Stream, had originally been a polo club for the Phipps family. In fact, during my first years there, ponies were still being trained on the sports fields. A little clapboard classroom was tacked onto some pony stalls to accommodate the children who had been plucked from their real schools up north to spend "the season" with their parents. The school finally outgrew the Polo Club, or vice versa, and Gulf Stream Polo moved to a more spacious location away from the sea.

In those years, highway I-95 was planned and built, Florida boomed, and I observed all that was quirky and magnificent about it. To me, Florida was part Flagler-era perfection, part George Merrick genius, part Lapidus moderne, and everything in between.

Palm Beach was, of course, Florida at its most magical. The Worth Avenue of my childhood was a true land of enchantment. It was where we shopped for special things: Luigi sandals and Florence Eiseman dresses from the Lullabye Shop. Fancy foreign shops were sprinkled among the resort boutiques. At Bettina di Capri my mother bought her skinny, long-sleeved cotton T-shirts. It was the Jackie and post-Jackie years, and Palm Beach women wore a sort of uniform of skinny trousers and skinnier cotton tops.

OPPOSITE Aldous Bertram's charming illustration of an Amanda Lindroth Collection raffia umbrella over a custom-printed, carnival-striped coral-and-white tablecloth from Quadrille.

And then came Lilly Pulitzer with her kaleidoscopically colored clothes. My father's campy green Lilly blazer crawling with turtles had its moment in the 70s but made its way into all four of his children's college wardrobes for "fancy dress."

There was the old Taboo, a pitch-dark restaurant even during the day, with giant glass grape chandeliers and thin Palm Beachers drinking martinis on banquettes in the shadows at lunch. There was the fancy French Petite Marmite, where our parents took us now and then and where tableside flaming service thrilled us. There was The Loggia, a 1940s pencil-reed-rattan-covered bar where we snuck drinks in our teens. Everything was so stylish—there was a lot to take in.

Had I known at ten years old that one could make a career in the style world, I might have gotten an earlier start. As it happened, a Wellesley education and jobs that included stints at WWD and W magazine, as well as PR for Gucci and other luxury brands, was my initial path. Though I never veered from my love and study of architecture and design, I didn't make it my business until I was in my forties.

The *Odelay*, a Hinckley belonging to a beloved client who trusted us to help with its décor. Seen here at the Sailfish Club in Palm Beach, Florida.

Returning to a "tropical" life by moving full-time to Nassau in my thirties, after living in New York, Paris, and London, rekindled the design ideals of my childhood. I started designing houses for myself, then for my husband's development company, and finally for clients here, there, and now everywhere.

A proper dose of Palm Beach was added when we let a 1928 Maurice Fatio apartment on Worth Avenue with soaring sixteen-foot ceilings in the summer of 2015. We soon gave it a mad, over-the-top painted chinoiserie interior. An office in Palm Beach completed the circle.

I am known for my island interiors. They derive from a lifetime of observation and study of the various ways those who live in tropical climates do it.

Architecture has been an invaluable teacher. When I was ten, my family moved to East Boca Raton and into one of the aforementioned Danish modernist houses that my mother helped design. The house was a far cry from any of the standard Florida idioms. It was good modern. It had perfect proportions and living in it taught me all about scale.

My mother's modern tropical aesthetic included all crisp white cotton slipcovered upholstery, China Seas batiks, Ward Bennett rattan-and-chrome Sled chairs, and the first Belgian wall-to-wall coir carpeting that anyone had ever seen. As children we were shocked by its scratchiness, but even then I knew it was chic.

I had given my mother what I would later understand was a mood board for my room in the new house. It included a tear sheet from a Marimekko advertisement and a detailed furniture plan.

In those early years, trips to Key West and the Bahamas started to nurture a love for tropical design. Though I have lived in Lyford Cay for almost thirty years, my very first trip here was in about 1972. My father's closest friend chartered a war-era taildragger DC3 and stuffed it with his children, stepchildren, soon-to-be new wife, soon-to-be more stepchildren, dogs, and bicycles.

His menagerie was decamping to a rented house in Lyford for the summer, and he invited us to join them for a day trip and lunch at the exclusive Lyford Cay Club. As soon as the plane landed, the children were instructed to ride the bicycles all the way to Lyford. I later understood this tactic was to evade the customs man. On the way, the only vehicle that passed us was our parents' taxi. It was the summer and the island was quiet and beautiful.

My first lunch at the Lyford Cay Club was served by waiters on a table made from the stump of a great casuarina tree. It was on the beautiful lawn between the cabanas and the sea. That was years before the Beach Shack was built for casual lunches on the dune.

This little tree table, where the children were sent so the parents could have a more civilized time at the Pool Terrace, was, I suppose, the precursor of "casual dining."

It would be fifteen years before I returned to Lyford for a year's stay.

An old-fashioned order still reigned in the community back then. There was a gentlemanly estate agent, Freddie Wanklyn, who had been appointed by Edward P. "Eddie"

A self-portrait of Aldous hard at work painting the mural in my Palm Beach apartment during the fall of 2015.

Taylor, the founder of the community. Freddie and his wife, Lu, were a dynamic duo who, if they thought you fit in, gently sold you a spot, introduced you, and generally made the whole thing work.

Within weeks of moving to Nassau, we had nothing but fun. it was a magical year of discovery and freedom. Nassau still had innocence. We drove our convertible VW to town for dinners. We went to the casinos all dressed up after parties in Lyford. We swam in the sea late at night, tipsy and enthralled by the beauty of it all. We were seriously young.

I discovered Harbour Island in the late 1980s. On our first trips there, we stayed with the Wanklyns at The Whale, their nineteenth-century house on Princess Street. The island was still largely pedestrian then. I do not even remember traveling in a golf cart. We went to South Bar for dinner in a taxi, our driver dressed in a customary tie and cap.

Freddie and Lu had amazing culinary skills. At breakfast on our first morning, a plan for the day was hatched. Freddie had secured a giant hogfish, which he placed in a bath of gently simmering water to poach all alone while the house party went to swim on a remote beach in Eleuthera.

By the time we returned at 1 o'clock, the giant fish was ready. Someone clever made homemade citrus mayonnaise and there were boiled potatoes and salad. The table had been set in the garden, and a long, very silly lunch ensued.

After lunch, Freddie had the table cleared, and all the dishes were put into a children's plastic pool, the type one would buy at a corner pharmacy in a coastal town. Dishwashing liquid was squirted liberally and the garden hose dowsed the lot. The simplicity and magic of that afternoon set a lifelong standard.

My decorating aesthetic was vastly influenced by these simple and perfect times. I learned to use what was available and handy. Pure cottons from the dressmaking department of the local Nassau fabric shops became my go-to textiles. There were bolts of seersuckers and checks and crisp cotton piqués—all delicious, fresh, and perfect.

On the cover of a recent *House Beautiful*, the dreamy eyelet bed hangings in a master bedroom I designed are

OPPOSITE Favorite pieces of correspondence and island ephemera from my desk at Hope Hill, including vintage stationery from the Royal Victoria Hotel and vintage Calypso records.
TOP A framed silk tourist scarf from the 1950s. We scour ebay for these scarves to frame or cover pillows.
ABOVE A thank-you note from an artsy friend after a silly Indian dinner with poppadoms at home.

fashioned out of five unnoticeably different fabrics. There simply wasn't enough of any one fabric, so we cobbled the various fabrics together, to no ill effect!

I have worked in Lyford for decades with the most talented, self-taught upholstery and drapery people. No doubt, some of the homespun solutions we have come up with would have been frowned upon elsewhere. We create lampshades out of straw work from the local straw ladies because of an alarming dearth of lampshades on the islands. And we spray-paint the card shades when they get marked or damaged. A found vintage rattan or wicker piece is relished no matter its state of disrepair. Love and paint go a long way.

The DNA of my island decorating has largely been dependent on the island-y complexities of availability, shipping, and climate. The builders of the Loyalist cottages on Harbour Island and elsewhere in the Bahamas were masters of understanding the local conditions. I love these old houses, and I have owned a few. I have learned a lot from living in them and apply that knowledge to the design of my clients' new houses.

We study cross ventilation, we look at wind, and we are very aware of the path of the sun during the year, as it affects the siting of a new house. Though we are old-fashioned, we use computer models to be sure our calculations of these conditions are accurate.

I want to live in, and I want my clients to live in, houses that have a cross breeze all year long. I want old-fashioned shutters, which mitigate uncomfortable light at sunrise and sunset. A house must stay cool in the hottest months and have dappled, comfortable light throughout the year.

These principles were fundamental to the nineteenth-century builders, and we insist on including them in the discussion of every project we take on. We are rare among designers in our insistence on these concepts. That said, we design houses for modern families with all the latest bells and whistles. At the same time, we decorate them with beautiful, timeless elements. Our interiors are known for basic straw mats on floors, limed cypress and pecky cypress walls and ceilings, and lots of art and books, all surrounded by beautifully designed tropical gardens filled with intimate and inviting places for outdoor entertaining.

ABOVE LEFT A beautiful detail of the Orchid Room dining space that we created for the Kips Bay Show House in Palm Beach. The honeycomb dome, scalloped orchid basket, and cane-wrapped glass hurricane are all signature products of the Amanda Lindroth Collection.
ABOVE RIGHT For a picnic lunch on the beach at Old Fort Bay, the table is set with Amanda Lindroth Collection placemats and block-printed napkins.
OPPOSITE Entertaining on the Lyford Cay Club golf course during the Lyford Cay Design Weekend, a biennial event with breakfast for two hundred at home! Amanda Lindroth Collection batik tablecloths and red goblets complement the seasonal bougainvillea centerpieces.

HOPE HILL

LYFORD CAY

Hope Hill has been our family home since 2010. The moment I laid eyes on it, I knew we would be happy there forever. The house was built by an American family in 1980. The name of the great lady of the house was Hope, and she had a razor-sharp eye and unmatched style. Under her command, Hope Hill was infused with whimsy, color, and charm. Her previous oceanside house in Lyford, Villa Contenta, was famously photographed by Slim Aarons. After a devastating clash with a hurricane, Hope decided to move to high ground and chose a spot on the top of a hill, due south from the front of the Lyford Cay Club.

Hope proceeded to plant the grounds with a jungle of tall, thin Alexander palms, which have soared to the height of the three-story house and now shade the verandas and dance about in the breeze.

When we bought Hope Hill, it needed a bit of a facelift. It had been designed in the late 1970s by the masterful Czech-born classicist Henry Melich, who designed all the best houses in Lyford at the time. In the 1970s construction was still very complicated on the island, necessitating shortcuts. Even many of the houses with perfect classical shapes had such idiosyncrasies as sliding aluminum "patio" doors, uninspired tile floors, and aluminum railings. Hope Hill was no exception.

As it was to be our year-round home, we decided to take the plunge and add the finishes that would give it a more Old World aesthetic. With the help of our frequent collaborators, Miami-based architects Maria de la Guardia and Teófilo Victoria, a husband-and-wife team who run DLGV Architects, we "Messelized" the house, incorporating all the wonderful idioms of the houses designed by Oliver Messel in Barbados in the 1960s and '70s. This entailed cladding it in cedar shingles, removing the three-foot overhangs from the roof, and adding all-wood windows and wide-plank floors. The house also got a full dose of the Messel whimsy in its railings and shutters. We debated the color for a long time, finally deciding on Benjamin Moore Southfield Green to mimic what is known as Messel Green in Barbados.

We added a few extra windows, raised the height of all the interior doors, and installed beautiful pairs of half-louvered, half-paneled interior doors. A Dutch door opening to the motor court welcomes visitors.

OPPOSITE For an early summer supper at Hope Hill, the table is adorned with flowers from the garden, and a rosé from Provence chills atop a China Seas Peacock Batik tablecloth.

The house has a wonderful layout: the family bedrooms are on the top floor and all the guest rooms are on the middle floor, nested in a jungle. Both levels have the benefit of a covered veranda that extends the entire length of the house. Shutters that reach from the ceiling to the top of the veranda railings can be closed in inclement weather. These shutters are the old-fashioned way to protect a house from the elements on the islands. On a windy or rainy night, they are easily closed, and the veranda becomes a room with just the right amount of breeze moving through the louver slats. During Hurricane Matthew in October 2016, these beautifully designed and traditionally made mahogany shutters protected the house from 165 mile-per-hour winds.

We eat all meals outside on the upper veranda. Breakfast is served at the western end, with the morning light filtered through the shutters. Extending from the veranda in the northeast corner of each level is an octagonal folly. Lunch and dinner are served in the upper Octagon. A pair of kestrels has nested in its soffit. There is often a bit of drama at lunch, when the parents come sweeping in to check on the chicks.

Hope Hill was built for guests and friends and entertaining. It is a perfect island house and our family treasure.

TOP LEFT The octagonal entrance pavilion at Hope Hill with its Messel Green parapet and lantern.
ABOVE LEFT Hope Hill's 1959 Fiat Jolly loaded for a picnic. Its pink sister Jolly gets more hits on Instagram!
ABOVE RIGHT In the pecky cypress–lined octagonal foyer, vintage Chippendale Peacock chairs sit below custom-made Raj Company mirrored brackets. The metal palm trees flanking the doorway were a consignment store lucky find.

ABOVE My ever-growing collection of Bahamian paintings find homes on easels and even on the floor.
OVERLEAF One end of the enormous drawing room is anchored by a Dutch walnut cabinet, a gift from a friend who found it at auction. Its provenance was a plantation on St. Kitts, and it came with a stack of photographs to prove it. A Bahamian policeman statue solves its slightly diminutive height. The wood tray ceiling, coralina walls, and shiny dark wood floors are all signatures of mine. Straw rugs, piles of paintings, blue-and-white-printed fabrics, and a well-stocked bar complete the layers.

ABOVE AND OPPOSITE The little multipurpose room off the kitchen serves as an office, breakfast room, and comfy TV-watching spot for my family. The make-believe Saarinen table doubles as a scheming surface on occasion.

TOP LEFT The four-poster bed in the master bedroom features an upholstered canopy. The room opens onto a terrace that overlooks a palm grove. TOP RIGHT Among the bits and bobs cluttering my dressing table are a shell bouquet purchased in the 1960s at the Red Cross Fair at Government House, Nassau, and a green enamel brush set from my mother-in-law. ABOVE LEFT The bed in a guest room features cotton eyelet and lace bed hangings and a block-printed spread. It sits on a striped cotton rug. This room, like all the guest rooms in the house, benefits from the dappled light created by a jungle of slender palms. ABOVE RIGHT This powder room is decorated with a jumble of vintage shell works assembled over decades.

ABOVE My daughter, Eliza's bedroom. The China Seas curtains were a present from her godfathers when she was born and have traveled to three different houses. OVERLEAF The magical veranda stretches the entire length of the house. It accommodates four tables of eight and seating for drinks, and we have even managed to set up one long table for fifty! All the furnishings are vintage wicker and receive a fresh dose of striped cotton fabric from time to time.

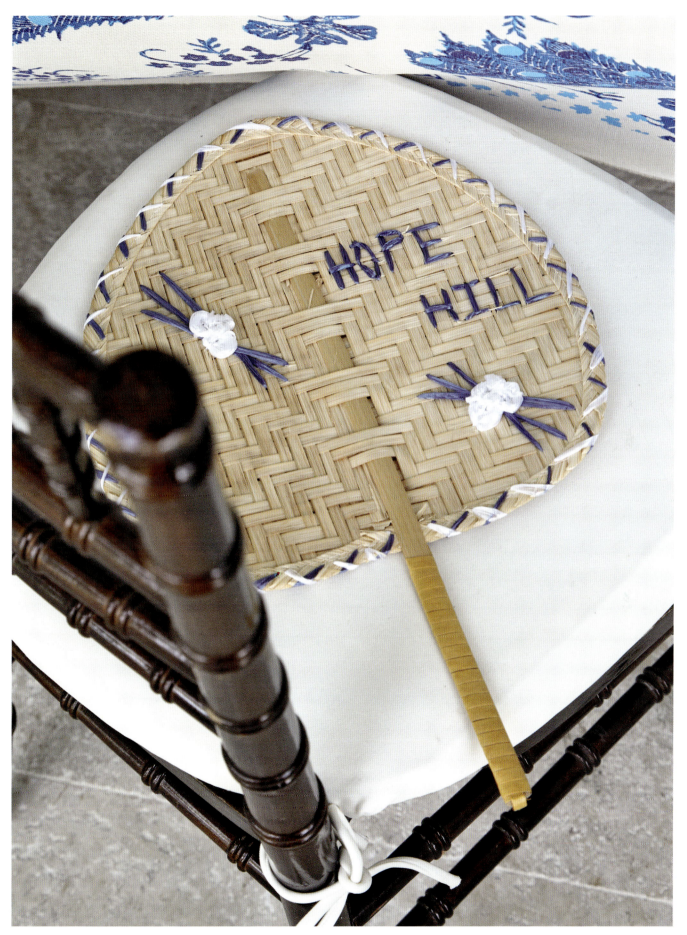

PRECEDING PAGES The old-fashioned working shutters can be closed to protect the veranda from wind and rain. A love of the houses of Oliver Messel in Barbados influenced the reconstruction of Hope Hill. We used Banjamin Moore's Southfield Green to approximate Messel Green, which was named in his honor. OPPOSITE A table set for supper includes Amanda Lindroth Collection straw mats, batik napkins, and bamboo flatware. A family silver mint julep cup keeps ice water frosty cool on a hot summer night. ABOVE Locally embroidered Hope Hill fans, a gift from a kind friend, come in handy when entertaining in the heat.

BAYVIEW
LYFORD CAY

From time to time there are dream jobs, and working on Bayview was certainly one of them. The clients, exceedingly private, uncommonly kind, and elegantly urbane, came to Lyford for an afternoon and bought a house and the adjacent lots. The scope of the project was to renovate the existing house over a summer so that it would be ready for occupancy by the winter season and to design and build a new house on the adjoining land. The schedule was aggressive.

Having a generous amount of land to work with, the architects Scott Merrill and George Pastor from Vero Beach, Florida, created a complex of buildings assembled like those on an English country estate. At the entrance to the property, there are gatehouses with guest accommodations. Along the winding driveway to the house are charming folly-esque structures. The drive culminates in a seagrape-lined motor court at the entrance to the house, which is flanked by the family's library complex on one side and the tennis and sports area on the other.

The clients wanted the atmosphere of the house to be calm and serene. Perhaps the most peaceful space is the U-shaped interior courtyard, which is dominated by a giant pink silk floss tree. This special tree was discovered in a yard in Florida by people whose job it is to drive around looking for botanical treasures in old gardens. I don't know the details, but I think they literally knock on doors and ask to buy wonderful trees.

In the foyer, the wide-plank teak flooring, salvaged from Harvard's Fogg Museum, has been hand-painted in a checkerboard pattern. The humble wood wainscot intentionally brings the grandeur down a notch. The family's beautiful collection of marine paintings hangs on the watermelon-colored walls of the living room. A wide green-and-white-striped tablecloth adds a bit of whimsy, as does the faux-tortoiseshell-painted armoire. A pair of stuffed peacocks rule over Kentian tables.

In the dining room, a Bohemian chandelier made for the Indian market hangs in a room paneled in limed pecky cypress. Inset in the paneling is a rare set of early nineteenth-century Dufour hand-painted wallpaper panels depicting Captain Cook's travels in the South Seas. The plate racks in the breakfast room were copied from those in a Swedish castle. The collection of antique Herend plates grows whenever we can find pieces at auction or on ebay.

OPPOSITE The bold pairing of watermelon and vibrant green lends a jaunty kick to this most magnificent of rooms.
OVERLEAF Bayview's sun-dappled, seagrape-lined motor court has a timeless appeal.

ABOVE Tall coralina wainscoting was added to give warmth to the entrance loggia. We hung mirrors above antique Italianate benches to reflect the mature landscaping. At the brilliant suggestion of our client, we painted the mirrors a happy coral.
OPPOSITE The painted floor of the foyer has buckled ever so slightly, betraying its age. The client and I were more thrilled than the builder when this happened! An antique rug and mirror complement blue-and-white porcelain and vintage tropical prints.
OVERLEAF Corner banquettes anchor the extremities of the 36 by 20-foot drawing room and create additional seating areas.

OPPOSITE, CLOCKWISE FROM TOP LEFT This French armoire was custom painted in a tortoiseshell finish and houses shells, prints, and a Victorian shell display under glass; Watercolors of shells hang above a Kentian carved table; A vintage French planter was whitewashed and its legs were cut off on site so that it could sit on the table; A detail of the corner banquette.
ABOVE At the center of the room is an awning-striped, mitered tablecloth surrounded by a set of exquisite Biedermeier chairs. A two-tiered antique chandelier with handsome Greek key ornamentation emphasizes the table's centrality. A pair of peacocks adds whimsy.

ABOVE An important Bohemian glass chandelier made for the Indian market hangs in the dining room.
OPPOSITE A special set of early nineteenth-century Dufour wallpaper panels depicting Captain Cook's voyages to the South Seas was purchased in New York. The pecky cypress–paneled room was designed around them. Vibrant coral linen upholstery adds a pop of color to the scheme.

OPPOSITE AND ABOVE The tiny octagonal breakfast room off the dining room has a soaring ceiling and millwork copied from a Swedish palace. The plate racks display the clients' collection of antique Herend plates and tureens. The hand-painted floors and hand-screened cotton fabrics contribute to the sophisticated simplicity.

RIGHT The family's sitting room is warmed up by Nobilis fauxbois wallpaper and overscale George Sherlock upholstered furniture from the U.K.
OVERLEAF LEFT The interior loggia, full of comfortable seating, plants, and shade, is an ideal space to spend afternoons protected from the sun. The handcarved consoles and mirrored planters were made in India.
OVERLEAF RIGHT At the center of the 100-foot-long veranda overlooking the sea, a series of tables with Delft-tiled tops have been set for a snack.

MINI SALT BOX
HARBOUR ISLAND

Harbour Island's worldwide appeal has grown exponentially over the last two decades. The international crowd is drawn to the three miles of pink sandy beach, the increasingly good food and shopping, and the charm of the nineteenth-century village architecture.

When Colonial America decided to get rid of King George III in 1776, a certain contingent of colonials sided with the king and came to the Bahamas with land grants and all their possessions. These folks became known as Loyalists. They settled in the Abaco Cays, Eleuthera, and various other Bahamian islands. Lord Dunmore, the last colonial governor of Virginia, then became governor of the Bahamas. His headquarters was Harbour Island, and the little island's town is named after him, Dunmore Town. Lord Dunmore was enlightened and laid the town out in a grid pattern with many well-placed, public accesses to the sea. Harbour Island's economy thrived on boat building, and the little working town burgeoned.

A century and a half later, Harbour Island became a popular tourist destination after the Pink Sands Hotel was built in the 1940s. It wasn't long before visitors started buying the charming village houses.

The early nineteenth-century Salt Box, owned by an English couple, is one of the oldest houses in Dunmore Town and one of only a handful of extant houses constructed of quarried local limestone. The couple soon bought the land next to the Salt Box with the intention of adding a small guesthouse—the Mini Salt Box—and pool. They chose the architect Kiko Sanchez to design the guesthouse after seeing his renovation of the Loyalist Cottage, which is thought to be the oldest house in the town.

The Mini Salt Box fits in seamlessly next to its elder sibling. Sanchez exactingly replicated its distinctive gable roof. Materials and colors were deliberately copied. A charming outdoor veranda serves as both living and dining room. Colorful cement tiles give some punch to the hall and the old-fashioned bathroom. Nothing about this new house looks new, and that was the whole point.

OPPOSITE A Parsons table and bench were made on site by a local Harbour Island builder. Agen chairs from Ikea—favorites of ours—contribute to the simple but inviting outdoor look.

Unique vintage high-backed rattan chairs from France, a built-in bench, and another homemade table comprise an outdoor living room. Louvered shutters can be opened and shut, depending on the weather.

TOP AND ABOVE An open-air mini-kitchen allows guests to make a drink or prepare a snack to enjoy on the veranda.

MINI SALT BOX ~ 51

ABOVE Hexagonal encaustic tiles in a variety of blue shades give this bathroom a whimsical yet timeless feel. Vintage rattan furnishings are in keeping with an old-fashioned bathtub. OPPOSITE This hallway connecting two identical bedrooms is adorned with hats and bags made by the ladies of Harbour Island, who do the best straw work.

OPPOSITE In one of the bedrooms, a Les Indiennes fabric enhances the bed and a locally made, fringed lampshade adds a touch of whimsy. ABOVE The other bedroom features a vintage bamboo-and-rattan desk and a dormitory-style black metal bed. The curtain fabric is from Les Indiennes. OVERLEAF The Mini Salt Box, designed by Kiko Sanchez, succeeds in capturing the spirit of its parent house next door, the nineteenth-century Salt Box, one of the most historic houses on Harbour Island.

WINDWHISTLE
LYFORD CAY

Windwhistle sits on the edge of the Lyford Cay Club golf course and has a sweeping view of the palm-fringed course. The owner, a great friend, inherited a wonderful collection of Bahamian watercolors and ephemera from her and her husband's families, who lived for decades in the Bahamas. Her late husband's mother built a house in Nassau in the 1920s. To say the couple amassed a lot of cool, rare Bahamiana would be an understatement.

When this house was finally renovated and the boxes began to arrive, it was like Christmas morning for a designer. There were hundreds of paintings of the Bahamas and rare black-and-white photographs, as well as beautiful shell work and coral.

Knowing that the living room walls would be covered with paintings I gave the room some form by anchoring it with two enormous carved, limed-teak cabinets. It was also a secret ploy to accommodate and display the owner's innumerable smaller treasures in an orderly way.

Most of the paintings that animate the living room walls are watercolors by Frederic Soldwedel (1886–1957). Soldwedel worked as an architect in Nassau for many decades and painted for fun—and to pay the bills, apparently.

His whimsical, charming works depict men climbing coconut trees, children swimming and diving for coins, men on Bahamian sloops racing in regattas, and other simple island scenes. Beautifully executed and delightful, his watercolors are also rare, and when any come up at auction in New York or elsewhere, we all secretly bid against our best friends to get them. Silly and true!

Windwhistle is also a great party house. With the doors on the golf-course side flung open, it has often been the setting of late-night dancing to the infectious sounds of Bob Hardwick's orchestra and candlelit dinners under the palms.

OPPOSITE Aldous's rendering of our client's hand-carved cabinet of curiosities, including a whimsical shell owl and other treasures under glass domes.

ABOVE A charming rococo-style overdoor welcomes the visitor to Windwhistle.
OPPOSITE A sampling of the eclectic collection of tropical arts and crafts in the Windwhistle foyer.

The walls of the living room and adjoining bar are covered with a diverse collection of Bahamian watercolors, drawings, and oils.

ABOVE One corner of the living room features a banquette and charming watercolors of boys swimming by Frederick Soldwedel. OVERLEAF The living room, with its coralina-lined walls and pecky cypress tray ceiling, reveals the client's love of the color aqua.

ABOVE A view down the grasscloth-lined hallway toward a portrait of a beautiful island girl.
OPPOSITE This stair hall artfully showcases the client's island and safari headgear, as well as other unusual objects, including a hexagonal sampler of local straw work.

ABOVE A pair of coral-painted headboards pops against bed hangings of Brunschwig & Fils' West Indies Toile. OPPOSITE Antique sailor's valentines surround a mother-of-pearl-inlaid mirror. OVERLEAF The Windwhistle pool in the early evening light, awaiting guests for a sunset cocktail. The exotic Balinese umbrellas provide shade in the late afternoon.

WATER MARTINS

LYFORD CAY

We had a call one day at the office to meet with a client about a house that was being redone in Lyford. The house had always been a bit of a mystery. It had been designed in the 1960s by the architect Robertson "Happy" Ward, perhaps best known for having founded the Mill Reef Club in Antigua. It had been owned by a very private gentleman who lived most of his life in a Lutyens country house in the Cotswolds. His infrequent visits to Nassau and the immaculate way the house was maintained added to the mystery.

When the elderly gentleman passed away, he left the house in Lyford to his charming young niece. Our new client arrived with great excitement to make the small house suitable for her young family. It needed a few extra bedrooms and a family room. It also needed new bathrooms and floors and all the other things that a fifty-year-old house in a salt-air climate requires. A proper re-do ensued.

We wanted the house to remain true to its 1960s heritage, so we searched for appropriate vintage pieces. We bought a rare pair of metal palm-tree mirrors for the living room, antique bamboo chairs for the front hall, and old aluminum Woodard Chantilly Rose chaises and curved sofas and chairs for the pool terrace. The giant aqua-and-white fringed Santa Barbara umbrellas poolside look like the Florida I knew in the 1960s.

Our client loved shopping for Bahamian straw work at the market in town, buying charmingly embroidered bags and hats on each trip. We matched her enthusiasm by installing a hat rack for her treasures in the entrance hall, the walls of which we covered in straw work and then silk-screened with a geometric print.

Upstairs, there was a new, awkwardly long hall, so we acquired a stack of matching faux-bamboo-framed mirrors from a defunct hotel in Daytona Beach and spaced them out along the walls on both sides of the hall.

The client's new second-floor master bedroom was spacious enough for an entire set of 1940s white-painted rattan furniture. We covered it in a 1960s China Seas hot pink chrysanthemum-print fabric, which seemed just the right vintage for the house.

OPPOSITE An outdoor shower comes in handy near the beach. This one is located between the pool and the golf-cart shed, a convenient stop for anyone heading toward the house after a swim.

ABOVE A Victorian bamboo hat rack holds the client's ever-growing collection of Bahamian bags and hats.
OPPOSITE Grasscloth printed with a geometric pattern plays off the geometrically patterned straw runners. A whimsical tall and thin Chippendale-style mirror punctuates the end of the hallway.

TOP An existing cabinet was repurposed as a bar. An abstract tortoiseshell pattern on the doors and a mirrored back infuse it with new life for its island setting.
ABOVE Island ephemera.

Antique maps are layered in a casual way atop the somewhat formal mantelpiece.
A pair of oversize sofas slipcovered in white cotton duck also softens the formality.

ABOVE Decorated with a vintage yellow mirror and a grouping of vibrant artwork, both original and reproduced, a powder room exudes casual charm. The sink is loosely skirted in a delicate print from China Seas.
OPPOSITE In a bay window overlooking the pool, a built-in bench covered in a colorful ikat makes an inviting breakfast nook.

OPPOSITE A William Skilling painting of birds in a cage was an incredible find. It anchors the family's game room and hangs over a vintage fiberglass rattan console. Giant elephant ear leaves introduce a vibrant green to the room's grasscloth-covered walls and bold Tashkent curtains from Quadrille.
ABOVE We gave vintage chairs a bright new color.

RIGHT The master bedroom was an addition to the house and therefore gave us the luxury of a large space to decorate. We installed a full set of vintage pencil-reed living room furniture and covered it in a China Seas hot-pink chrysanthemum print. The pretty eyelet bed hangings, gathered at the top in a feminine way, complete a very old-fashioned feeling in a brand-new space. Overleaf We hunted down these 1960s Woodard Chantilly Rose chaises in thrift shops, consignment stores, and on ebay. They were powder-coated in a soft aqua and placed under a pair of two-tiered, fringed Santa Barbara umbrellas. Wild banana trees flank the seating area.

THE DUNMORE

HARBOUR ISLAND

From the day Gil Besing, owner of the Dunmore Hotel, rang me in January 2009 to discuss working on this little treasure, I knew it would be a great project. What I did not know and could not have appreciated then was the Dunmore's widespread appeal. People young and old, from near and far, love this property and place. Why it is so loved is partly obvious, partly inexplicable, and largely owing to factors that have less to do with decorating than with its many layers and elements, which, taken together, make it such a magical place.

The credit really goes to Gil, who let us assemble an incredible team. Maria de la Guardia from DLGV Architects in Miami was there from the start. The building was in poor condition, but because it was our desire to repair it rather than replace it, Maria had cause to wonder what her contribution would be. When her plane landed back in Miami after her first walkabout on the property, she rang me and said, "If the Dunmore falls down and I am the architect, do you think I will lose my license?" I giggled.

Maria diligently drew new footings and did whatever else needed to be done to secure the broken little building in the sand. We debated at length whether the original jalousie windows should stay or go. Our decision to keep them was counterintuitive, as jalousies are universally vilified as a bad moment in window design, but for some reason they just seemed right.

The tiny Clubhouse needed to be redesigned to serve not only as the reception area and bar but also as a dining and living room. Because the Dunmore is such an ineffably charming place, this task, which should have been hard, was not. It all works, and the room is cheerful during the day and sexy enough in candlelight at night.

When we reviewed the overall plan, we all agreed that the property lacked an "arrival moment." The inconvenient truth was that the obvious spot for it was occupied by a small building that housed the entire resort's electrical and mechanical equipment. Gil's flawless instinct was to spend the considerable sum necessary to move the equipment, allowing us to build one of my favorite buildings ever. The entrance pavilion is a tiny breezeway with a pair of shed roofs. It says you have arrived but with such subtlety that it is a mere tickle. It is also a rain-free area for a luggage drop or to wait for a taxi. From this pavilion, one wanders down a narrow, jungle-y path to the Clubhouse. The first glimpse of the turquoise sea pops up over the rooftop. It is perfect. And it is one of my happiest professional achievements.

OPPOSITE The Dunmore's iconic aqua-and-white umbrellas have been the hotel's signature on the pink sand beach for forty years. It was therefore natural for us to complement them with a striped towel shack at the foot of the dune, where guests can grab the necessary gear for a day on the beach.

ABOVE My very favorite building in the Caribbean, this tiny pavilion flanked by two shed roofs creates the arrival moment at the Dunmore. A wisp of a structure, it nevertheless has great presence.

When I saw this demilune banquette, I could picture it in a 1960s discotheque in Palm Beach. Its quirky, unusual shape made it perfect for the foyer of the Clubhouse.

BOTTOM RIGHT We designed the cabinet behind the reception desk to serve variously as room-key holder, display board, and cabinet of curiosities. Ersley Wilson carved and painted this distinctive sign; others can be found all over the property.

OVERLEAF The fireplace and flanking bookshelves, filled with novels left behind by guests, create a cozy reading nook. Plenty of comfortable seating covered in plain cotton fabrics makes reading and cocktailing alike possible day and night.

OPPOSITE AND ABOVE Dozens of old photographs of Harbour Island and other Bahamian islands, a few old album covers (records still inside), and the odd locally found shell all combine to make this one of the most photographed rooms in the Caribbean. The jaunty coral, tangerine, and white stripe became the iconic Dunmore fabric, and we used it wherever possible in this tiny but magical Clubhouse.

ANGLER'S COTTAGE
GREAT ABACO

Sometime in about the 1970s, the Bahamas Ministry of Tourism started to encourage the use of the term *Family Islands* for what had previously been called the Out Islands—all seven hundred islands and cays in the archipelago except Nassau and Grand Bahama. On the narrowest part of the Family Island of Great Abaco sits a three-mile-long stretch called Schooner Bay. Its unique position, with the vast, mangrove-dotted shallows known as the Marls for fly-fishing on one side and the Atlantic Ocean for deep-sea fishing on the other, makes it a dream locale for avid anglers, particularly bonefishermen.

The owner of this cottage is one such angler. The little house, situated with views of the harbor on one side and dramatic, rocky Little Bridge Beach on the other, has a sporty, Out Island vibe, evident in its relaxed decoration. It is an upside-down house, with its living and dining areas on the second floor to take advantage of the island's wonderful crosswinds.

Practicality in the Family Islands is a must, and we deliberately use hardier fabrics and materials when decorating in these somewhat remote spots. The more rugged decorating perfectly suits the rugged nature of the place. To play up the relaxed environment of this house, we removed the doors from the kitchen cabinets. Vintage bits and pieces give the little cottage a timeless quality.

Verandas top and bottom on both sides offer safe havens from sun and wind, depending on the quickly varying weather conditions. Schooner Bay is truly a magical dot of a village in a vast, open, pristine area. As there are no other communities nearby, the nights are cloaked in darkness. The verandas provide comfy spots for gazing at the star-studded sky on these dark nights. The starlight is one of the things that astounds all visitors to Schooner Bay.

OPPOSITE This modest cottage is owned by an avid angler who takes full advantage of Schooner Bay's ideal fishing conditions.

ABOVE Shiplap ceilings, coralina floors, and dark wood stairs are the traditional materials of Abaconian architecture.
OPPOSITE On the second floor, the living room boasts dramatic views of Little Bridge Beach.

ABOVE Vintage French rattan chairs and a pair of pedimented cabinets made of reclaimed barn wood give the living room a textured feel. OPPOSITE A long trestle farm table is just right for family dining in the open air.

OVERLEAF Kitchen cabinets were designed without doors and were painted the blue of the sea and sky for dramatic effect. PAGES 102–3 LEFT AND RIGHT The house's unique position in an extraordinary natural environment between two rugged coasts at Schooner Bay.

HAVEN HILL

LYFORD CAY

When Ashley, one of my closest friends and my daughter's godmother, called to say that her family had bought a house in Lyford Cay, we all jumped for joy at the thought that she and her husband and children would be spending more time in the Bahamas. We had a mere eight weeks to get the house ready. I should not say that Ashley granted us carte blanche, but because we're such close friends, she essentially said, "Go for it." We just had to try to stay on budget and meet the deadline.

The house had great bones, but there was not enough time to address the windows and bathrooms—they had to wait. We painted kitchen cabinets, some tile, and even a bathtub! And we wallpapered to our hearts' content.

In the living room, we painted some rather fancy trim black so it would disappear. We found the best vintage curved rattan sofa we had seen in years and upholstered it in crisp white to pop against the mad navy palm-motif wallpaper. For fun, we added another print to the room—a hot-off-the-presses China Seas peacock print.

For the living room we bought a beautiful Soldwedel oil of the Bahamas at auction in New York. It was later joined by a pair of Tom Scheerer–designed bookcases from the couple's New York apartment. They fit the space like a glove.

The adjoining dining room got a crazy Mario Lopez Torres chandelier. The room had fancy paneled walls, which we mirrored and trimmed in the smallest-print navy batik wallpaper we could find. The couple shipped down a Saarinen dining table, which sits on a geometric-patterned dhurrie.

In the master bedroom, we layered corals and pinks. The colors stand out against a sea of green from the golf course and the palm fronds that are at arm's length from the bedroom's terrace.

When the couple and their three social, sporty, college-aged children are in town, the outdoor terrace serves as the venue for lively dinners. The house's shutters are painted the same green as those at Hope Hill, so we often share vintage metal party chairs, which are painted the same color. They get taken back and forth between our houses on golf carts.

The pool is in an elegant sunken area down a slope from the house and is surrounded by tall walls of flowering bougainvillea.

Haven Hill shares its name with a family house in Massachusetts.

OPPOSITE An overscale Mario Lopez Torres chandelier teeming with birds and monkeys presides over a Saarinen table in this mirror-paneled, Melong Batik–trimmed dining room. Grounding it all is a Jonathan Adler cotton dhurrie.
OVERLEAF In the living room, Cole and Sons Palm Jungle wallpaper, black trim, China Seas Peacock Batik fabric, and the best vintage rattan sofa we have ever come across combine to make it madly whimsical.

TOP Green zebra stripes and Indian block prints give this twin bedroom punch.
ABOVE Block prints on the wall and on the bed envelop another guest room.

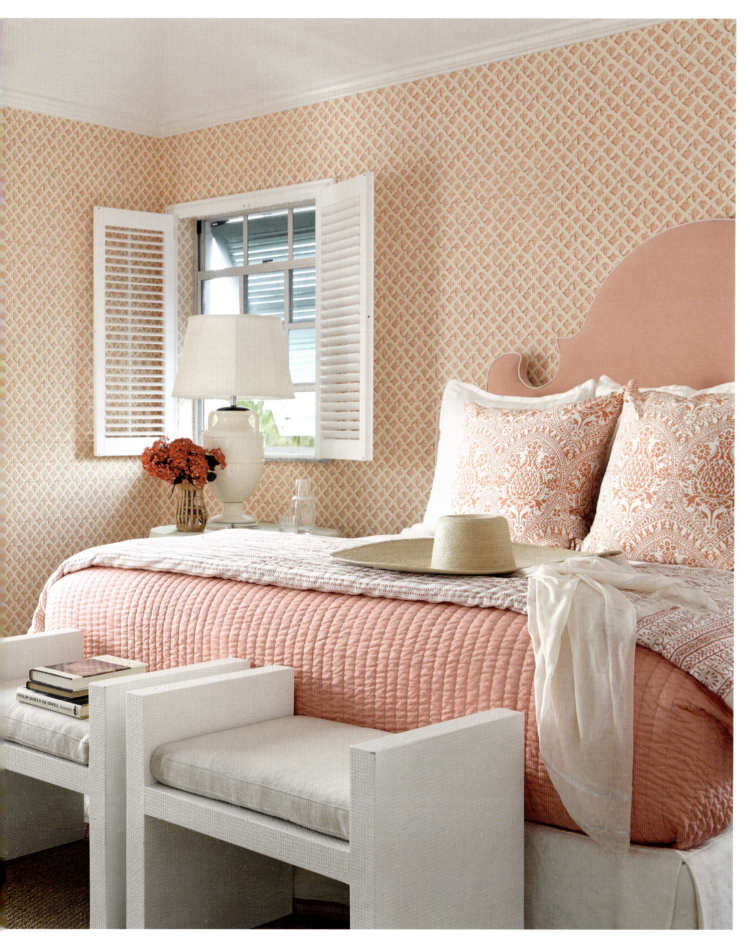

Layer upon layer of pink prints create a fresh Lyford Cay look in the master bedroom.
A pair of 1960s Parsons benches anchors the foot of the bed.

LEFT Painted and natural rattan pieces are unified by pink linen cushions and pillows covered in China Seas batiks. The oversized mirror is from Dimond Home. The shutters are painted in my favorite Messel Green.
ABOVE A sunken, walled pool area is enveloped in bougainvillea to magical effect.

MOON STONE FARM

LYFORD CAY

It is not often that a decorator gets a commission to design a barn on a tropical island. In this case, the client's mandate was clear. She wanted the barn to be a highly functional place for her family and friends' horses and other animals, flanked by two wonderful apartments where the family could spend weekends. The setting is a farm featuring a wonderland of exotic chickens, rare plants and trees, an abundant vegetable garden, an orchard, meandering trails, and a lake.

The family is famous for its pizza parties. These candlelit evenings are held out under a jade-green, vine-laden veranda. The host and hostess serve yummy homemade pizzas baked in a wood-burning oven that is based on the one in their family's house in Provence.

For the style of the barn, the client instructed us to think more gypsy caravan than British Empire. After all, even the horses stabled there are not ordinary Thoroughbreds but the horses of the Romani. Small and round with beautiful manes that are combed and braided with ribbons, they pull hand-painted carts all about the place.

For the flanking apartments, we looked in a few directions. On one side, we tented a bedroom à la Charlottenhof. The client's children were young teens at the time, and we thought it would be fun for them. In the living area, we added a collection of finely woven rattan exotic animals on brackets. And we covered the client's French chairs in the same tenting stripe.

On the other side, we created a serene place for our client to spend the afternoons riding, working, and relaxing in solitude away from her main house, a ten minute golf-cart ride away. We furnished the living area with comfortable upholstered pieces, built pretty bookshelves, and lined the walls with Catesby prints of the flora and fauna of the Bahamas. Mark Catesby documented the natural world of the Bahamas, Florida, and the Carolinas a hundred years before Audubon. The Queen has the original drawings at Windsor, but the special early prints turn up from time to time, and we try to acquire them for our clients.

OPPOSITE A row of basket pendants dangles from the jade-green shed-roofed veranda of the barn, a shaded area for dining, doing puzzles, or just relaxing after a ride.

ABOVE The client's own puffy French bergères were covered in tenting stripes to give them an informal look.
OPPOSITE TOP A collection of finely woven rattan animals was found at F.S. Henemader in Palm Beach and mounted on brackets above a giant down-filled sofa in one of the two apartments flanking the barn.
OPPOSITE BOTTOM In the other apartment, framed Catesby prints of birds of the Bahamas cover a wall.

ABOVE Simple metal beds from Ikea and a whimsical drum chandelier from Carlos de la Puente Antiques in New York feel at home in this attic bedroom, tented in the style of Charlottenhof Palace in Potsdam, Germany. OPPOSITE For the bedroom in the other apartment, we chose a more romantic bed and draped it in a sheer John Robshaw block print, which we trimmed in pink cotton. OVERLEAF Our client's distinctive style is as evident in her penchant for Gypsy, rather than Thoroughbred, horses as it is in the use of three shades of green for the veranda of her barn. Chairs from Ralph Lauren and Ikea blend seamlessly.

SPURLING POINT

GREAT CRANBERRY ISLAND, MAINE

When we got a call to meet with a young couple to discuss designing their new house on Great Cranberry Island in Maine, we had no idea that a week later we would be on a ferry, braving sub-freezing temperatures and a stiff wind in mid-winter to make the crossing from Northeast Harbor to Spurling Point.

I had come from Nassau via Boston, and I don't even own the kind of winter garb that can keep one alive in conditions like this. Not to mention that this part of Maine is closed for business in February. The heat is off, the boats are out of the water. The place is a snowy ghost town.

But upon our arrival at the house, we were struck by its magic, even in the middle of winter. It is in fact quite famous. Just about everyone who summers in these environs passes it on the various water journeys to and from the islands that make up this summer community. The previous owners had entertained regularly and lived beautifully in it. Their dinners were legendary; even I had heard about them in Nassau. The interior was appointed with beautiful polished-chintz fabrics, shirred polished-cotton lampshades, and charming wallpapers.

Our clients wanted to give the house a very gentle facelift, respecting all that was legendary about it. Our mandate was to make it wonderful for them and their beautiful young children, all three under six! As this was Maine, we did what is natural in these parts. We saved furniture we could re-use, we bought treasures online, and we revitalized pieces from our clients' other residences.

We reserved our splurging mostly for fabrics. Our clients loved the cottons of Les Indiennes, Pierre Frey, Carleton V, and Peter Fasano. Using these hand-printed fabrics seemed like just the right way to freshen a grand dame whose previous attire had been polished chintz.

We also had a bit of fun finding a pair of fiddlehead wicker chests of drawers and then matching headboards. The fiddlehead motif just feels so right for an attic children's dorm room in Maine.

It is our hope that this young family will have years of delight at Spurling Point.

OPPOSITE A watercolor rendering of Spurling Point, on Maine's Great Cranberry Island. Spurling Point is spectacularly sited, boasting unrivaled views of Acadia National Park across the water.

A corner table in the great room at Spurling Point takes advantage of the ocean view through open French doors.

A mixture of family pieces, Indian prints, and vintage rattan creates a cozy environment for the young family.

ABOVE AND OPPOSITE To give the library a warm, inviting ambience, we covered the walls with Nobilis faux-bois wallpaper and chose a fuzzy Moroccan rug.

The clients' beautiful portrait of an Indian warrior inspired the pops of color in the small dining room.

TOP A pair of fiddlehead chests of drawers was the starting point for this large attic bedroom with its tester beds and matching fiddlehead headboards. ABOVE Sweet China Seas fabrics imbue this bedroom for the family's two young girls with delicate charm.

We dressed a bay window in the master bedroom with simple ice-blue linen curtains and valances. The pine ceiling and wainscot were painted a fresh, glossy white.

LA PALOMA

LYFORD CAY

To say that the owner of La Paloma, located a stone's throw from the Lyford Cay Club, is one of the most elegant women of her generation would be an understatement. She is a great beauty, even regal, and a ton of fun. Lucky for us, she asked us to decorate the new house for her.

She explained to me that she had been coming to the Lyford Cay Club since she was young. Every year, her parents took the children to the same clubs and hotels around the world for their holidays. They never had a second home. When she and her husband and children decided to buy a house in Lyford, she wondered, "Would owning something here ruin it for us?" We knew that our job was to make her feel at home. And that meant giving the house a club-like atmosphere, specifically the Brighton Pavilion–type glamour that is so evident at the Lyford Cay Club.

In the foyer we covered the walls in Lyford Pagoda, printed on grasscloth in a bold Lyford coral. We sprinkled vintage Ficks Reed rattan pieces throughout the interior, including a one-of-a-kind mid-century settee. This little settee had caught my eye a year before I found the perfect client for it. I have never seen another one before or since. Above it hangs a giant Serge Roche–style palm mirror.

In another just-like-Lyford moment, we copied Tom Scheerer's handsome lantern-like chandelier. The maker made me get written permission from my friend Tom, who was responsible for the renovation of the Lyford Cay Club, before I could order it. I must say I applaud the firm for that. For the bedrooms we used a palette of the softest pastels, just like the guest rooms at the club.

Our client feels right at home at La Paloma.

OPPOSITE China Seas' exuberant Lyford Pagoda wallcovering, printed in coral on grasscloth, greets the visitor in La Paloma's foyer.

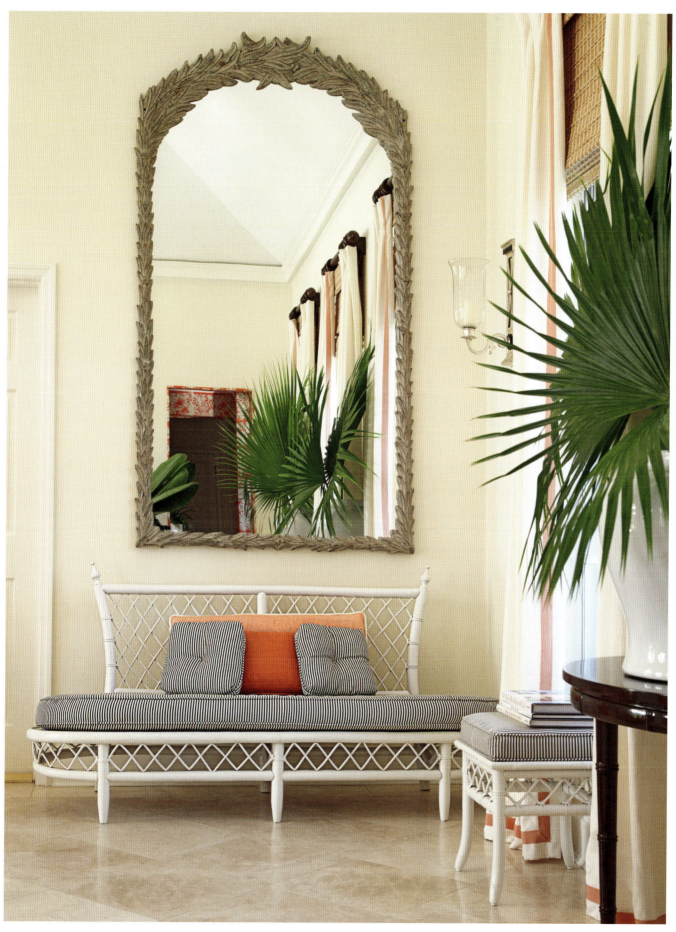

OPPOSITE The Lyford Pagoda pattern carries through to the grand living room, where it covers a pair of armchairs.
ABOVE A unique Ficks Reed settee adds vintage charm to a corner of the living room. Above it hangs a Serge Roche–style palm mirror.

ABOVE A 1950s high-backed chair gives the house a dash of Lyford pink. Botanical prints of palm species in driftwood frames hang above it. OPPOSITE The dining room is furnished with vintage finds from the antiques shops on Dixie Highway in West Palm Beach. The lantern chandelier is a replica of a Tom Scheerer design.

Circular mirrors hang above a pair of vintage faux-bamboo metal beds in a guest bedroom.

The serene ice-green color of the master bedroom's walls is an homage to the color used in many of the Lyford Cay Club's guest suites. The pretty China Seas fabric gives this room an airy feeling.

BIENESTAR

PALM BEACH

Jealousy is an ugly trait, but when our clients rang us to tour their pied-à-terre in a 1920s Marion Sims Wyeth masterpiece, known as Bienestar (Spanish for "well-being"), in the heart of Palm Beach, I had to catch myself. The house is hidden amid a jungle of vegetation and hedges on a secret road one block from the beach.

As it turns out, a brilliant developer, Robert Eigelberger, divided this beautiful estate into six "apartments" in the 1980s. Though it could have resulted in a mess, it ended up being a perfectly wonderful group of residences that happily coexist in a wild garden. Think Paradiso Perduto, the overgrown Florida mansion in the 1998 movie version of *Great Expectations*, starring Gwyneth Paltrow.

Our clients, luckily, got the portion of the house with the grand front door. In its original iteration, the door opened onto an open loggia. Now that loggia is our clients' main hall and dining room. We softened its pecky cypress ceilings with a touch of lime to create the subtlest palette for their amazing collection of modern art.

To stand up to the power of the art, we made floor-to-ceiling red-and-white-striped curtains. And for a touch of whimsy, we had shirred and flounced red ceiling pendant "lampshades" made.

In the living room, a plain sheetrock ceiling felt a bit sad and unloved. We added a 1920s-era pecky cypress ceiling to be "friends" with the one in the loggia. We boldly stenciled it in a cobalt-blue paisley pattern.

As the house is nestled in a magical garden, we worked with the landscape architects to create a great seating area, a special spot in the garden for dinners, and a place to barbecue. We designed an oversize awning to accommodate the vintage Woodard semicircular sofa. We had it powder-coated in the same soft green as the window frames—an homage to Palm Beach architect Addison Mizner, whose green windows imitated the patinated-copper windows of the Old World.

This project has Old World charm, New World art, and everything enviable in between.

OPPOSITE This space, originally an open loggia in this Marion Sims Wyeth residence, now serves as the main hall and dining room. Three oversize red shirred-cotton pendant lampshades impart a dramatic sense of scale, as do the floor-to-ceiling red-and-white-striped cotton curtains with black trim.

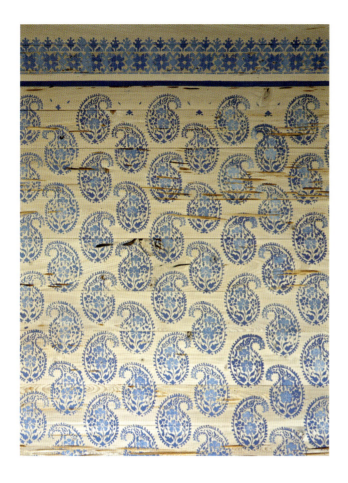

OPPOSITE In the living room, an overscale English ottoman and layers of blue-and-white prints resonate with the stenciled ceiling. ABOVE, CLOCKWISE FROM TOP LEFT The ceiling was clad in pecky cypress, which was then stenciled in a paisley pattern to create a unique effect; Hand-carved chairs and consoles lend a rich elegance to the scheme; An exceptionally beautiful hand-carved chair graces the hall; Books, shells, and flowers add visual interest.

OPPOSITE In the under-stair powder room, Quadrille's Happy Garden wallpaper references the antique tile on the stair risers.
ABOVE Giant six-foot-tall blue-and-white soldier jars add a surprising moment in the lush garden. We painted a set of Phyllis Morris Chinese Chippendale-style chairs a mint green to match the windows of the house.

ABOVE We designed an oversize awning with Moorish detailing to create an outdoor living room. The 1960s Woodard semicircular sofa was found on ebay and painted mint green.
OPPOSITE The residence's original, beautiful 1920s courtyard.

PALMETTO HOUSE

LYFORD CAY

When our clients bought Palmetto House, their intention was to clean it up for a few seasons' use and then tear it down and start afresh. But after we learned that the house had been designed by legendary Palm Beach architect John Volk, we hatched a new plan: to recapture the whimsy and style of Lyford Cay during that early era.

First we added apple green–painted louvered panels liberally through the house. The green also made its way to the original Volk bookcases, which flank the fireplace in the tray-ceilinged living room.

Our brief was to use mid-century furniture—a new vernacular for the owners and for me. A Danish modern pedestal table stands at the center of the large living room. On either side of it is a seating group anchored by a vintage rattan "pretzel" sofa and Adrian Pearsall mid-century slipper chairs found on 1st dibs. In an area nearby, a mid-century low, upholstered sofa is grouped with vintage rattan chairs from a yacht.

To set the Lyford mood in the children's identical bedrooms, we covered the walls in matching palm-motif wallpaper, pink for the daughter's room and blue for the son's.

We found a palmetto-frond wallpaper in black for the little rooms flanking the entrance foyer, one the powder room and the other the tropical version of a mud room, where tennis racquets, golf clubs, straw hats, and other Lyford Cay essentials are stored.

To give the front façade of the house a bit of a flourish, we dressed it in striped awnings and dramatic curtains. The Palmetto House sign was hand painted in a style inspired by the iconic signage of the Beverly Hills Hotel.

OPPOSITE We painted the original built-in bookcases a glossy apple green to make them pop. "Pretzel" rattan sofas and an amoeba-shaped coffee table are in keeping with the mid-century pedigree of this John Volk–designed house.

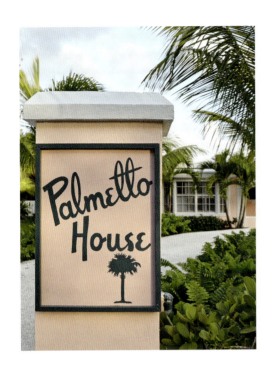

OPPOSITE, CLOCKWISE FROM TOP LEFT The Palmetto House sign was painted in the font of the Beverly Hills Hotel; Stripes and bold curtains lend flair to the front of the house; In the large living room, apple-green louvered panels were added to break up the space, and vintage hooded chairs, splashes of orange, and a Danish modern center table complete the retro look. ABOVE A Keno Brothers writing table displays favorite books. Vintage rattan chairs from a yacht flank a 1960s sofa. A custom cocktail table from Harbinger in Los Angeles sits in the middle.

TOP Pink-and-orange Palm Shuffle wallpaper from Wallshoppe gives a daughter's room a shot of tropical color. A stripe in the same colors from Ralph Lauren was used on the cushions of the miniature wicker barrel chairs.

BOTTOM LEFT A palmetto-frond wallpaper was magically found to cover a pair of rooms flanking the foyer: a powder room and, seen here, a mud room.

ABOVE The blue colorway of the Palm Shuffle wallpaper is complemented by a corresponding stripe in the son's room.

OLD FORT BAY CLUB

OLD FORT BAY, NEW PROVIDENCE

Certainly one of the most special buildings on the entire island of New Providence is the Old Fort. When pirates were wreaking havoc in the Bahamas in the eighteenth century, the British built a simple battlement on this spot at the edge of the beach. After those troubles ended, the Old Fort became a sisal and rope plantation.

In the 1920s the property was allegedly won in a high-stakes card game at Bradley's in Palm Beach. The winner's family added the Mediterranean details to the building. The taste for Spanish Colonial architecture was prevalent in Palm Beach at the time.

Lunches and dinners with the Cuttings, who owned the Old Fort in the 1940s–1960s, were renowned. Mr. Cutting was known as a gentleman explorer, and he had lunch served under Tibetan tents. The Old Fort was left untouched for the next forty years, until 2003, when we restored it for use as a small private club.

In the forty years of its "benevolent abandonment," the Old Fort's beautiful two hundred-year-old giant silk cotton tree, English cannons, and faded murals of local boating and fishing scenes, painted by Stephen Hawes, a guest of the Cuttings, were the subject of wonder.

Generations of beachgoers told the same tale of wandering up the beach, scaling the wall, and discovering this hidden, overgrown fort. It even had a bat cave.

The Old Fort's transformation into a club was an effortless task. Its magical spaces were easily converted into a bar/drawing room, library, terrace, and dining veranda. Dining at night under the giant silk cotton tree is illuminated by no fewer than a hundred candles lining walkways, staircases, and every other appropriate spot.

The Old Fort Bay Club has become an essential and integral part of life in western New Providence. Families congregate there for the beautiful beach and the wonderful atmosphere. It is still very Old World, just as any eighteenth-century fort that has been repurposed for the twenty-first century should be.

OPPOSITE A watercolor rendering of a picnic table set up on the beach at the Old Fort Bay Club.
OVERLEAF In our transformation of Old Fort into a club, we gave the walls of the bar/drawing room an atmospheric, aged feeling. Bar furniture is easily moved around to accommodate members as they come and go on busy nights.

The outdoor dining terrace at the Old Fort Bay Club overlooks cannons that are directed toward a channel where pirates and other buccaneers made mischief in the eighteenth century.

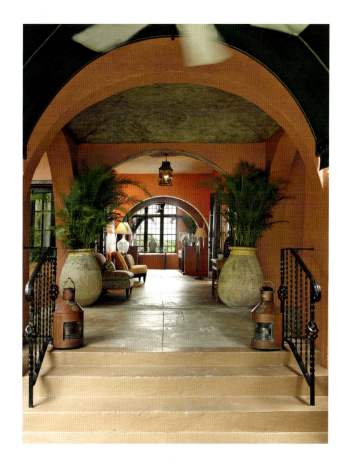

TOP The entrance hall at the Old Fort Bay Club.
ABOVE One of the restored murals that were painted by Stephen Hawes, a Beaux-Arts-trained English painter who was a guest of the Cuttings, the owners of the place in the 1940s–1960s.

OPPOSITE Details of the Old Fort Bay Club exterior. The canopies of 200-year-old silk cotton trees shade the Colonial-era buidings. ABOVE The steps leading from the club to the beach.
OVERLEAF A table is set for a picnic under the palms on the incomparably beautiful Old Fort Bay beach.

SCHOONER CABANA

GREAT ABACO

My very favorite beach structure, the Schooner Cabana, was designed on a loose piece of paper, at lunch, by a master, or rather, a couple of them. Teófilo Victoria, the great classicist from Miami, and his architectural collaborator, my husband, Orjan, have a long history of returning from their favorite sushi boîte in Coral Gables with a sketch or two.

The sketch for the little pagoda-shaped, thatched-roofed cabana appeared after just such a meal, and we knew we had a winner that would be perfect for Schooner Bay, a newly planned harbor village on Great Abaco. Orjan, who conceived and developed Schooner Bay, futher embellished the cabana with wonderful details and nuances, shielding it from the sun with just the right shutters and positioning window openings in just the right spots. The cabana is elementally perfect, a 16-by-28-foot building that in my opinion is the best beach structure created for our climate in a century.

When developing Schooner Bay, Orjan and Teófilo assembled a team to design its plan. Headed by Andrés Duany and Elizabeth Plater-Zyberk of DPZ, leading proponents of New Urbanism, the team created the first New Urbanist plan for a "Family Island" in the Bahamas. The plan draws on the design of eighteenth- and nineteenth-century Bahamian villages such as Dunmore Town on Harbour Island, Hope Town on Elbow Cay, and New Plymouth on Green Turtle Cay. Schooner Bay's plan achieves the perfection of the old—nothing intrusive or out of scale.

A cottage near the cabana is equipped with all the bells and whistles of modern life in a tiny format. The traditional cottage, which has two bedrooms and two bathrooms, is owned by Antonius Roberts, an artist and a Bahamian national treasure. His sketches hang above a 1820s-era sofa in the living area.

OPPOSITE For the walls of the Schooner Cabana, we decoupaged and antiqued maps, then mounted them in bamboo frames to create the look of a found antique collection.

OPPOSITE A view of the thatched-roof cabana from the water.
ABOVE The Schooner Cabana's tiny flanking service pavilions are nestled in a palm jungle.
OVERLEAF The cabana serves as an artist's studio. The beautiful and wild Atlantic is but steps away.

ABOVE The diminutive drawing room of an artist's cottage near the cabana. The handsome lines of an 1820s American Empire sofa—an ebay find—lend an air of sophistication. Antonius Roberts's beautiful sketches are hung from a brass chain system that allows the artist to change the selection at whim.
OPPOSITE The windows of this seating area are unglazed to take advantage of the island's prevailing breezes.

OPPOSITE In the drawing room, small club chairs are slipcovered in crisp seersucker. Old barometers sit atop the handmade console. ABOVE The master bedroom is simply furnished with a vintage faux-bamboo metal bed and hand-blocked cotton linens.

LILY PAD

HARBOUR ISLAND

Alongside the Dunmore Hotel on Harbour Island is a small, perfect oceanfront parcel of land where our client, the owner of the Dunmore, asked us to help design a few houses. With Maria de la Guardia as the project architect, six houses were planned and built in the same old-fashioned idiom as the Dunmore. All were designed with the wind and sun patterns of Harbour Island in mind. They offer shade at the correct time of the day and breezes and cross ventilation throughout the day.

For this house, we wanted only old things. We hoarded masses of antiques and quirky vintage rattan, as well as lots of old Bahamian maps and art. When the containers landed and all the mismatched pieces were being unloaded, our team looked despondent. Everything was vintage and in perfect scale, but it all needed love, paint, polish, and repair.

So the team got to work painting, polishing, and reupholstering, and the house came together. The success is all in the quirky bits: a pagoda-shaped rattan daybed, decoupaged maps of the islands in vintage round rattan frames, a blue palm-patterned wallpaper for the kitchen. This new house looks old and just right next to the Dunmore.

OPPOSITE A whimsical vintage rattan pagoda-shaped daybed is a perfect place to nap. Its striped curtains hide an outdoor television. Various vintage Ficks Reed rattan chairs flank an Oomph cocktail table.

ABOVE A view of Lily Pad from the motor court. Messel Green abounds.
OPPOSITE The entrance foyer has a vintage beachy theme. The round map of Eleuthera reminds visitors where they are and echoes the medallions in the frames of the almost-matching mirrors.

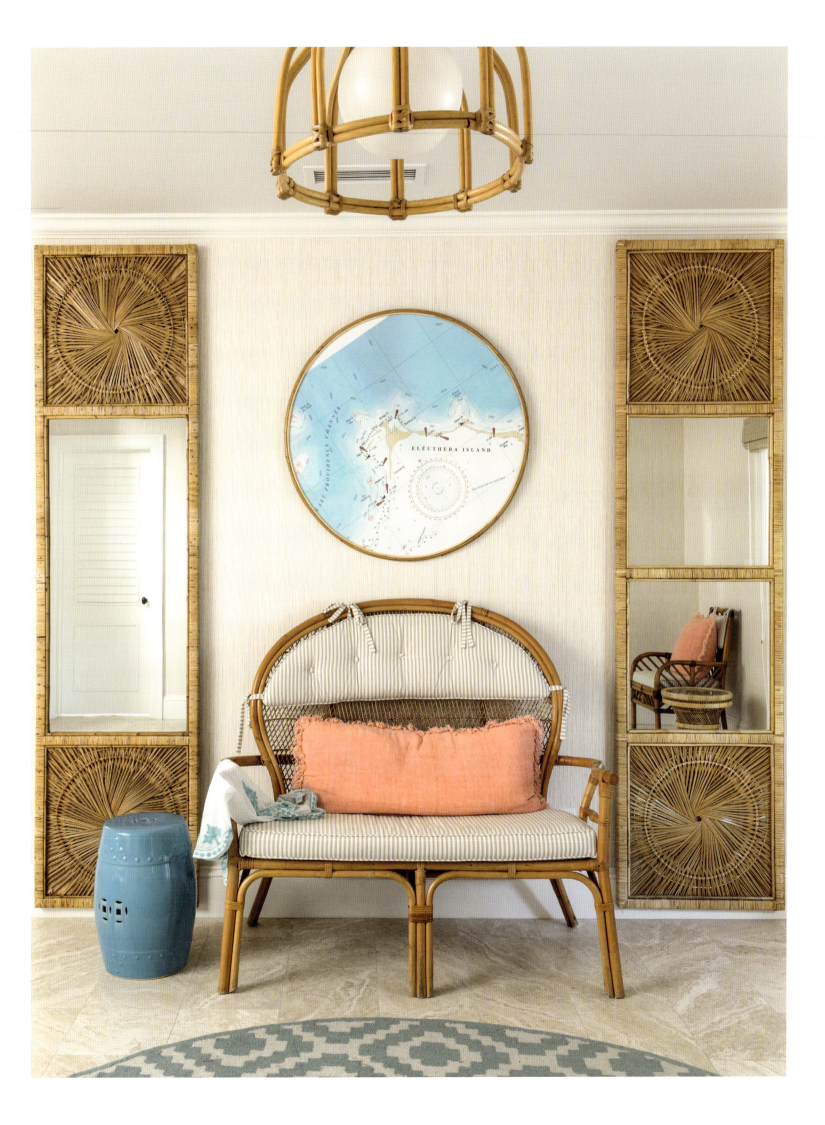

OPPOSITE The beautifully proportioned second-floor drawing room with its soaring shiplap tray ceiling combines living and dining in this upside-down house.
ABOVE Cole and Sons' Palm Jungle wallpaper adds a touch of whimsy to the kitchen, as do the vintage elephant-shaped wicker side tables, which we painted black and repurposed as plant stands.

TOP A pink, geometrically patterned dhurrie grounds this guest room.
ABOVE When the antique Indian four-poster bed we ordered for the master bedroom arrived, it was so tall that we had to cut down the legs on site.

A mélange of geometric patterns, a blue and aqua palette, and maps painted by Bahamian artist William Johnson combine to give the children's bedroom a cheerful vibe.

OPPOSITE The Messel Green shutters are echoed in the giant two-tiered, scalloped, and fringed umbrellas.
ABOVE Our favorite Agen chairs from Ikea, painted Messel Green, sit on the upstairs dining porch.

COMPASS POINT
ANTIGUA

Imagine our delight when we were asked to travel to Mill Reef to do a few upgrades on a beautiful house originally designed by Robertson "Happy" Ward. Ward was a legendary architect who had offices in Barbados, Nassau, and Bermuda. He was also the founder of Mill Reef in Antigua.

Happy Ward searched high and low in the 1940s for a spot in the Caribbean to build a retreat for his friends and other like-minded souls. Mill Reef's atmosphere then, and to some extent now, was relaxed and informal. There were no Saturday night black-tie dinner dances. Houses were restricted in size and cost. There was meant to be a sort of utopian level playing field. Status was earned by the quality of the rum punch recipe that each household concocted.

Compass Point sits on the top of a mountain overlooking the incredible little volcanic island Green Cay. The view is dramatic. The wind and the salt spray at Mill Reef are unrelenting throughout the year. The houses take a beating. In addition to upgrading the house, our client at Compass Point wanted a fresh start for the cottage on the property, so it was torn down and Maria de la Guardia designed a new two-bedroom cottage and pool, as well as an outdoor living room that extends from the cottage on the side away from the wind.

All materials had to be hardy to withstand the conditions. Inside and out, we used limed Indian teak furniture, made for us by the Raj Company in India. We layered batiks and hand-screened fabrics. The look is timeless, and the cottage appears to have been there since the Happy Ward days.

The garden was redesigned by Cecilia de Grelle. The landscaping envelops the house and cottage, creating plenty of carefully thought-out nooks and crannies for friends and family to lounge in. Mill Reefers famously start the day with visits to friends' houses for a rum punch. It is known as the Noon Balloon there. Sounds like fun!

OPPOSITE The dramatic, commanding view of Green Cay from the Compass Point terrace, high above the Mill Reef Club.

OPPOSITE The charming arched bar with blue shutters, seen from across the courtyard.
ABOVE Stools inlaid with bone and a hand-carved Indian table add texture and a touch of the exotic to the open foyer.

ABOVE In the new guesthouse, a teak-and-cane daybed made in India is available for napping or an unexpected visitor.
OPPOSITE The beds in one of the new guest suites were designed with the client, who found a beautiful palm motif for the inlaid bone. Layers of hand-screened and hand-blocked blue-and-white Indian fabrics complete this suite.

OPPOSITE The Indian theme carries through the other guest suite, which is decorated with Indian prints and cerused, hand-carved beds. ABOVE Details of the Indian-made furniture and objects in the second guest suite.
OVERLEAF The newly constructed infinity pool extends to the edge of the highest point of this magnificent hilltop site.

TOP AND ABOVE Two views of Compass Point's garden terraces. OPPOSITE A huge, curving sofa inspired by an image of one in an Agnelli residence was made in India to fit this spot.

CHICCHARNEY
LYFORD CAY

Chiccharney is a mythical Bahamian creature, like a gnome, I think. I have never really known much about these make-believe creatures except that they are reputed to live in the caves and nooks and crannies that make up the coral formation of the Bahamian archipelago. It is odd that this wonderful house, which has had three glamorous female owners successively, should be named after a cave creature.

Chiccharney House was built in the 1960s for Annie Orr-Lewis, the woman who singlehandedly created the "Lyford Style." A supremo tastemaker, she was a very close friend of the founder of Lyford Cay, who let her loose on its interiors, allowing her to set all the style standards. She decorated many of the original houses in Lyford and went on to have a career decorating residences and clubs throughout the region.

There are Slim Aarons photos of Orr-Lewis at Chiccharney, surrounded by her signature wicker basket seats, Portuguese painted furniture, and cotton fabrics. The next owner was another great doyenne of style, taste, and looks whose pink clothes, interiors, and lipstick were legendary.

Our client, who is young and beautiful, is the third owner of Chiccharney. She commissioned us to freshen up the house and give it a full facelift: new kitchen, bathrooms, windows, and floors. It was important to her that we retain all the Lyford idioms that had been introduced by the previous owners.

To this end, we kept all the cypress accents, retained lots of the original wicker and rattan, and gave the Brown Jordan Calcutta outdoor furniture a fresh coat of blueberry paint. We added lots of layers of batiks from China Seas, fresh cotton and jute rugs, and a giant Scott McBee painting of crowned cranes in the living room.

Chiccharney now has its third successive style doyenne in residence. Not many houses can boast such a thoroughly stylish pedigree!

OPPOSITE A watercolor rendering of a fabric-backed bookcase.

ABOVE Scott McBee's oversize painting of crowned cranes on a fuchsia background makes a vibrant backdrop for the living room.
OPPOSITE TOP Chaises longues on the upper terrace have a sweeping view of the Lyford Cay Club and golf course.
OPPOSITE BOTTOM A pair of Chippendale Peacock chairs adds some scale to the double-height living room.

ABOVE A pair of generous rattan daybeds offers places to relax or read on the house's indoor-outdoor loggia.
OPPOSITE In the sitting room, we used China Seas' Persepolis to upholster the sofa and, for a bit of fun, the back of the bookshelves too.

OPPOSITE In the master bedroom, an antique Indian bed is layered with white-on-white hand-blocked cotton batiste.
ABOVE Details in the master bedroom include mid-century pendant nightlights and curtains with giant pom-pom trim.

TOP A pathway through the jungle leads to the pool. ABOVE Christopher Farr Cloth's Carnival Outdoor fabric animates a vintage club chair.

ABOVE We painted vintage Brown Jordan Calcutta aluminum outdoor furniture a cheery blueberry.
OVERLEAF A view of the charming Chiccharney from the garden.

TREE HOUSE
LYFORD CAY

In the summer of 2010 Orjan and I bought a forlorn little treasure of a house called Tree House in Lyford Cay. It sat on a giant double lot full of mature trees on the highest ridge in the cay. As it turns out, the founder of Lyford, Eddie Taylor, built the house in the early days to show potential buyers that the ridge had beauty too. Designed by a Florida architect, Tree House is one of the few mid-century houses in Lyford. It has sliding "patio" doors, 1950s awning windows, and low-slung porches and rooflines.

The house had been owned by a reclusive grande dame of sorts. The pantry was stacked with beautiful dishes, and the garage had Babe Paley's 1959 Fiat Jolly, which Lyford legend says had been a gift to her from Gianni Agnelli.

The house needed all new everything: bathrooms, kitchen, roof, and floors. We had recently sold another house and had a crazy deadline to complete the renovation before the school year started. Because of the time crunch, we sourced virtually everything we needed locally. The result was a fanciful house full of our cache of collected artwork and vintage finds.

The sunroom, which consisted of a super-flawed addition tacked onto another bad addition, posed a problem, so we tented the ceiling in striped canvas to hide the chaos. We cobbled together cotton eyelet from the dressmaking department at the local fabric shop to make the bed hangings for the master bedroom. I bought all the bolts of blue-and-white-striped and -printed fabric I could find to cover furniture and pillows.

The speed decorating worked, and as the crowning glory, we installed a beautiful infinity pool amid the mature gumbo limbo trees. Now the house on the highest spot on the ridge has regained all the magic that Eddie Taylor promised to those early buyers.

OPPOSITE A built-in bookcase, original to the house, and benches offer an insouciant way to display a large collection of Bahamian watercolors and oils.

OPPOSITE A 1940s oil painting of Nassau Harbor by Stephen Etnier hangs above an original cypress and faux-bamboo fire surround. Nineteenth-century watercolors of Nassau by Gaspard Le Marchant Tupper surround the painting.
ABOVE A beloved shell-filled backgammon table doubles as a spot for coffee and a perusal of the local paper.

The low-ceilinged master bedroom was given floor-to-ceiling corner screens covered in a bold Indian ikat to raise the eye. Similarly, the bed hangings were suspended from the ceiling to maximize the space. We upholstered the Ming-style stools in a local seersucker.

OPPOSITE In the sunroom, a tented ceiling covered the sins of a few awkward renovations.
ABOVE A little Parsons desk, with drawers open for extra space, makes a perfect corner bar in the sunroom.

ABOVE The Tree House gets its name from this quirky porch, which is built around a huge gumbo limbo tree that supports large staghorn ferns. OPPOSITE The infinity pool we added is surrounded by gumbo limbo trees and poincianas.

MAHOGANY BAY

BELIZE

I remember many moons ago seeing a *60 Minutes* segment on Belize. The reporter described the country, formerly British Honduras, as "high on spirit and low on paint." I was unsure what to expect when we jumped on a few planes to check out our new project there in 2015.

Beth Clifford, a super-talented and driven American developer, has created Mahogany Bay, a village on Ambergris Caye, a little island that is a ten-minute plane ride from the airport in Belmopan, Belize's capital. *60 Minutes*' gritty warning is apropos until one arrives at Mahogany Bay. Clifford assembled a team led by architect Julia Starr Sandford and her partners at StudioSky to build a new community with waterfront cottages and a monumental Great House for gathering. The result is a perfectly fresh take on a Caribbean idiom. The all-white village uses the old island language of shed roofs, jalousie windows, and metal roofs, but it has combined them in a new way that looks entirely original.

One of the secrets is that the houses are largely prefab, built off-site in a factory that Clifford set up in the forest on the mainland. Belizian hardwoods are world famous, and the team has perfected building in a variety of species. The houses float their way to Ambergris Caye on barges and are tilted up and assembled in a jiffy.

Our task was to design the interiors of the monumentally scaled Great House. For the wide and generous verandas, we combined high-backed benches made of local hardwoods with low-slung wicker and rattan seating.

For the interior, I imagined the grandest hotel in 1930s Tegucigalpa or some other Central American capital. We designed a matching pair of monumental wood units for opposite sides of the lobby: one serves as the bar; the other, as reception. We furnished the center of the lobby with large-scale sofas and vintage high-backed rattan chairs. As luck would have it, a large quantity of them happened to come across my desk at just the right time in the project. It is rare to be offered two dozen vintage matching rattan parlor chairs, but it was obviously meant to be.

OPPOSITE A watercolor of the pool area at Mahogany Bay's Great House.
OVERLEAF The grandly scaled veranda of the Great House.

TOP The reception area of the lobby in the Great House features one of the two monumental wood units we designed for the cavernous room.
ABOVE Detail of the Great House lobby.

We furnished the bar and seating area of the Great House lobby with large-scale sofas and vintage high-backed chairs.

CA'LIZA

OLD FORT BAY, NEW PROVIDENCE

After three years of dreaming, drawing, and making all the necessary arrangements, ground was broken on Ca'Liza on September 27, 2005.

There must have been a cosmic aligning of the stars because the first shovel in the ground happened on the day my daughter, Eliza, was born, just across the Gulf Stream in Miami. That amazing coincidence was not the reason we called the house Ca'Liza, after the Venetian idiom for naming houses (*ca'* is short for *casa*, or "palace"). We had chosen the name long before to honor our soon-to-be-born child.

Old Fort Bay, the 1000-acre plot just to the east of Lyford Cay, has arguably the prettiest beach on New Providence, the island on which Nassau, the capital of the Bahamas, is located. Both Lyford and Old Fort are at its western end. Ca'Liza has the prime position on this beach. Occupying the highest spot, it boasts sweeping views.

When my husband, Orjan, and his partners were developing Old Fort, I made a case to build a house for ourselves on its most beautiful lot. He agreed, and we designed Ca'Liza together with our longtime collaborators Teófilo Victoria and Maria de la Guardia of DLGV Architects in Miami. Ca'Liza won a Shutze Award from the Institute of Classical Architects in 2010.

The lot was challenging. It is more than 400 feet deep but less than 100 feet wide where it counts—facing the view. Our vision was to create the narrowest, palm-lined driveway for those 400+ feet. The drive was dotted with a few needed outbuildings, including a mother-in-law's cottage (for the dowager Mrs. Lindroth), a little schoolhouse, and a pair of garages with staff quarters above.

The entire exterior of the house and much of the interior, including columns, pediments, jack arches, and overdoors, are covered in quarried coral stone from the Dominican Republic, known there as coralina. Forty containers of coralina arrived at the site, to be unloaded and set in place like a great big puzzle.

Ca'Liza's many perfect attributes include verandas both upstairs and down that provide protection from sun and wind. All the verandas have louvered doors that can be closed, turning them into bona fide rooms. We had no need for curtains in the master bedroom because the doors on the veranda could be shut with ease, which we did every day just before sunset.

OPPOSITE Ca'Liza's seaside veranda is clad in coralina and has tall, louvered French doors.

ABOVE AND OPPOSITE The coralina-walled drawing room features all of my favorite elements: white cotton slipcovers, straw rugs, and vintage rattan.

Ca'Liza's ideal proportions, 52 feet wide by 52 feet long by 52 feet high, a perfect cube, explain its classical grace. It references Palladio's Villa Pisani in many respects. I once asked Maria why I feel different and happier in any room, house, or space she has designed, and her reply was quick, "You feel different because it is all about math and proportion. These calculations are based on classical rules."

Maria, Teófilo, and Orjan have long embraced the need to build things for the ages, just as Palladio did. With its timeless beauty, Ca'Liza makes a perfect companion to the historic Old Fort next to it.

ABOVE In the foyer, an early nineteenth-century Venetian mirror hangs over a hand-carved Indian console that is flanked by vintage Ficks Reed planters. OPPOSITE The walls of the dining room are clad in whitewashed pecky cypress. The dining table and chairs are Venetian. We covered the chairs' silk damask upholstery in white linen for an airy, more tropical feeling.

ABOVE The soaring, whitewashed-cypress tray ceiling in the master bedroom called for an extra-tall four-poster bed, which we draped in linen hangings. OPPOSITE A pair of armchairs upholstered in China Seas' chocolate Lyford Pagoda fabric flanks a custom-made, extra-tall, pagoda-style cabinet that balances the sky-high bed.

OVERLEAF A watercolor of the loggia on the garden side, a frequented spot when the wind is prevailing from the northeast.
PAGES 232–33 The house's ideal Palladian proportions are especially evident from the beach below.

L'ORANGERIE

LYFORD CAY

L'Orangerie is one of Lyford Cay's most beautifully designed houses. Everything about it, from its windows and doors to its shutters and hardware, has long been a source of study and inspiration for me. The story goes that a New Orleans family commissioned the architect Myrlin McCullar to design a new house in Metairie, Louisiana, a hotel in Little Rock, Arkansas, and L'Orangerie in Lyford, all in the same year—about 1970.

L'Orangerie's interior, originally decorated by Mark Hampton, was intact until just a few years ago. But when the termite-ridden legs of the club chairs began snapping off, our clients asked us to come and freshen up the place.

In the pretty main living room, we retained the Hampton furniture plan, although we supersized the pink sofa along one wall to create additional seating. We based the color palette on the rather beautiful paintings that were already in the room. The result is a cheerful, very Lyford Cay look. We threw in several rattan-wrapped étagères by Bielecky Brothers and geometrically patterned China Seas pillows as an homage to Mark Hampton. A cotton-and-jute rug hand-woven in Guatemala covers the floor.

In the main bedrooms, we maintained the traditional feel of the house, adding hand-screened fabrics and cotton-and-jute rugs. In the original house, most of the bedrooms were on the ground floor, except for one odd, nearly windowless bedroom upstairs. A previous owner had added bedrooms and bathrooms galore in the attic, and the house can sleep plenty of children and grandchildren now. L'Orangerie has been and always will be one of Lyford's most magical houses.

OPPOSITE The view of beautiful Clifton Bay from L'Orangerie's garden gate.

OPPOSITE Christopher Farr Cloth's pink Palma fabric enlivens these club chairs in the drawing room.
ABOVE An extra-long pink sofa and pillows covered in a variety of cotton prints give the drawing room its playful, happy feel.
OVERVIEW The drawing room's beautiful architecture, columns, and proportions are enhanced by the client's art collection and Mark Hampton's original seating plan.

OPPOSITE A geometrically patterned coral-and-pink dhurrie echoes the pattern in the wallpaper and the palette of the pillows and coverlet on the antique Indian bed in one of the bedroom suites. ABOVE A serene sky blue gives this guest room a particular freshness. The beautiful original French doors lead to the garden and beach.
OVERLEAF The pedimented loggia facing the pool is painted in the signature soft pink of Lyford Cay.
PAGES 244–45 The house's location overlooking Clifton Bay is unparalleled.

POINT OF VIEW
HARBOUR ISLAND

On Harbour Island there is long, bumpy road that leads to a strip of land that has always been known as the Narrows. Arguably the prettiest terrain on the island, it features palm-covered dunes and lush tropical vegetation on both the seaside and the bayside. The houses, nestled in the foliage, are largely obscured from view. The road to get there may be treacherous, but the residents like it that way.

Point of View is located just about at the end of the Narrows. It sits tucked back on a high plateau overlooking the bay and Eleuthera in the distance. It is not an old house, and our mandate was to add some touches that would make it feel more like Harbour Island's traditional village houses. To accomplish this, we first hand-painted all the floors. We chose wide concentric rectangles in a subtle beige and white for the foyer and a checkerboard pattern in the same tones for the adjoining living room. For the master bathroom, we "borrowed" the look of Bunny Mellon's floors in her Antigua home—a geometric pattern in a soft blue and gray-blue that has been slightly brushed for a worn feel.

For the furnishings on the ground floor, we went entirely vintage. The large, semicircular rattan sofa in the living room was an ebay find. We bought it from a farmer in Ohio who drove it to Ft. Lauderdale for us. The chairs facing it came from France. A monumental plaster mirror that we found in Hudson, New York, hangs over a tall-backed rattan settee in the foyer. Upstairs, the bedrooms are dreamy; the beds are draped in linen hangings and the floors are covered with cotton rugs.

As the clients are sporty and spend much of their time outdoors, we enlisted Maria de la Guardia to design a pool and pool pavilion, which we set off to the side so as not to impede the views across the lawn to the water.

The porches surrounding the house are dotted with amusing vintage hooded chairs and double sofas for napping. The porch on one entire side of the house serves as the "water sports department." Paddleboards and sails and other equipment are stored there, awaiting each day's adventures. We arranged a giant seating area on the lawn for parties.

Point of View has a point: It is a perfect family compound for sport and relaxation in the most idyllic setting imaginable.

OPPOSITE A palette of aqua and white lends a soft freshness to the children's bedroom at Point of View.

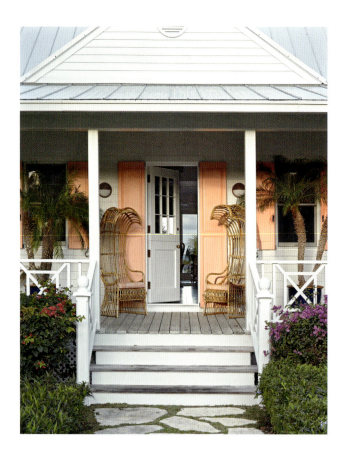

ABOVE Views of the exterior of Point of View. Vintage hooded chairs abound. OPPOSITE A giant faux-bois mirror hangs above a vintage high-backed rattan settee in the foyer, where the floor has been hand painted in concentric rectangles. OVERLEAF The furnishings in the living room are all vintage. We found the semicircular rattan sofa online, and the chairs were flown in from Denmark.

ABOVE The crisp linen bed hangings in the master bedroom add a touch of luxury to this island house.
OPPOSITE The master bathroom's hand-painted floor was inspired by the floor treatment in Bunny Mellon's famous house in Antigua.

The new pool pavilion and cabanas were intentionally designed to look like they had always been there.

GOOMBAY

LYFORD CAY

When a young family from Texas bought a house in Lyford for weekends and holidays, we were asked to make it cheerful and fun. The house had previously been the main residence for a couple, and it contained offices and both formal and informal entertaining spaces. The pair had been gourmet cooks, so there was a chef's kitchen.

To satisfy our clients' desire for a total change, we started by using a vivid orange for just about everything. To say the community was on the fence about the bold orange-and-white-striped awnings we added to the exterior would be an understatement. A few people gently asked, "What were you thinking?" Others expressed their opinion less gently. We proceeded undeterred, installing front and garden gates specially made in our bright color by Accents of France. We threw in about a million orange lanterns from Oomph and some orange-and-white fringed umbrellas too. The house is a splash of wonder and fun.

For the inside, we had Accents of France line all the walls of the foyer in treillage painted a minty green. We used Nobilis faux-cypress wallpaper in other rooms to warm then up.

The floors throughout the house were covered in terra-cotta tile. It would have been too costly and traumatic to pull up all the tiles, so we took a leap of faith and painted them. In the foyer they are green and white to complement the trellis. In the living room they have been carefully brushed, using a technique that approximates walnut parquet.

Everyone in the family is a sports lover. For the family room, which had previously been the dining room, we had the Raj Company stain two large, hand-carved cabinets in our orange tone: one to house the bar and the other to accommodate a giant TV. There is an equally enormous sofa and ottoman to make gatherings for sports events cozy. I am very envious of this setup.

Bedrooms got an equal dose of brilliant color. We furnished the upstairs veranda with vintage rattan daybeds for napping. Downstairs, the verandas are set up for dinners and parties. The large lawn was intentionally left bare for impromptu field games.

The community has stopped commenting on the bright color. Most have jumped on board and love it. After all, the house is called Goombay, which is a local word for music, festivity, and fun!

OPPOSITE Beautiful treillage by Accents of France envelops the foyer.

ABOVE We transformed a tiny hallway on the upstairs landing into a colorful, inviting spot to watch TV on this extra-long sofa. OPPOSITE Lining this hallway with vintage panels and mirrors turned it into a shimmering space. OVERLEAF A custom-made abaca rug grounds the vast living room, and voluminous white linen curtains with shell trim softens it. The clients' love of purple is seen in the choice of throw pillows.

OPPOSITE At the other end of the living room, we covered "pretzel" rattan chairs in a China Seas batik. Pairings of Kentian mirrors and tables add a touch of grandeur. ABOVE An enormous hand-carved cabinet with wave and shell motifs houses the bar. The extra-long blue sofa and striped ottoman can accommodate the whole family.

OPPOSITE The house's signature orange explodes in the master bedroom. ABOVE In the master bathroom, we blithely carried through the orange theme on a pair of Chippendale-style mirrors.

ABOVE The second-story veranda runs the length of the house and offers countless places for napping, reading, or taking in the Bahamian sunset. OPPOSITE Orange-and-white-striped awnings were added to all the exterior windows at Goombay. The bold color scheme carries through to the scalloped and fringed two-tiered umbrellas. OVERLEAF The back façade of this plantation-style house, seen from the pool.

WORTH AVENUE

PALM BEACH

One sleepy summer Saturday morning in Palm Beach, Orjan and I were having breakfast at the Surfside Diner. I was reading the wonderful monthly real estate magazine with the pretty watercolor cover that has been a staple publication in Palm Beach forever. A total stranger approached and asked if we were looking for real estate in Palm Beach. I replied that I wasn't but that I couldn't break the habit of checking out the listings. Earlier that day, in fact, I had mentioned to Orjan how happy I was staying at the Colony Hotel on my visits to Palm Beach. As it happened, this nice new friend said she had a wonderful apartment to show us and, sure enough, by noon that day we had agreed to take it.

Imagine an apartment with sixteen-foot-high ceilings right on Worth Avenue overlooking the swaying palms and stylish shops. With its Moorish windows and wood floors, it was simply irresistible. The building was designed in 1929 by Maurice Fatio, and our apartment, we believe, may have originally been a roof terrace. The transformation from terrace to apartment was done on a shoestring sometime in the 1960s, we think. Asymmetrical doors and a host of other silly quirks abound.

I enlisted artist and friend Aldous Bertram to give it a fantasy Palm Beach look. The inspiration was the wonderful Cecil Beaton watercolor of William and Mona Harrison in the chinoiserie drawing room of their Palm Beach house in 1937.

Aldous worked for three months. He dangled from scaffolding and painted away. For the fanciful overdoor ornamentation, he drew inspiration from the wonderful plaster overdoors at Claydon House. He emulated swirls found on Worth Avenue architecture. He even added legendary Palm Beach architect Addison Mizner's monkey, Johnnie Brown. The result is a whimsical bit of heaven.

The room is anchored by a giant, hand-carved teak cabinet. Aldous added the chair rail and used faux-bois wallpaper to simulate wainscoting. The room is outlined in a cork tape that Aldous found at a Michaels craft store.

The apartment has been our home away from home and occasionally the site of a dinner party for sixty in the courtyard below. We have never really been sure that we are allowed to dine in the courtyard, so we set up late and take it all down before bedtime. The tenuous nature of the party's legality adds to the fun!

OPPOSITE A Chippendale-style mirror and wicker settee were painted black to pop against China Seas' Rio wallpaper in the entrance vestibule. OVERLEAF Cecil Beaton's 1937 watercolor of William and Mona Harrison in their Palm Beach drawing room was the inspiration for this room. Aldous's painted interpretation of their antique Chinese wallpaper incorporates palms and banana leaves, slender pink marble obelisks, and parrots perching on blue-and-white vases. The eclectic mix of vintage furniture was all sourced locally, including Palm Beach's beloved Church Mouse.

OPPOSITE Details of the wall decoration include the fanciful overdoor, based on the plaster chinoiserie overdoors at Claydon House in England. Applied grasscloth panels highlight a stunning set of Palm Beach–themed collages by Jean-Charles de Ravenel. ABOVE A wicker table base was converted into a gigantic lampshade; a string of shell necklaces wraps around its chain.

A supersized tropical display rests on a large, square, skirted table, flanked by a pair of armchairs covered in a yellow Quadrille fabric. The trompe l'oeil stone scrolls replicate those on the famous clock tower at one end of Worth Avenue.

Only one of our signature giant carved-teak cabinets by the Raj Company could have had the stature to anchor this long, originally empty, wall. Aldous disguised asymmetrical doors and mirrored niches with riotously busy trompe l'oeil plasterwork, niches, shells, and ginger jars.

OPPOSITE In the master bedroom, Aldous's jaunty palm motif on the aqua walls and a Stark leopard rug generated so much energy that we opted for calm white fabrics. We used a dainty eyelet for the hangings on the vintage bed and upholstered the box spring in a vintage batik. My mother's portrait with Ribbons the dog has found its own special spot. ABOVE A giant apple painting from my childhood home was the starting point for Eliza's pink-and-green bedroom with its vintage French bamboo beds.

ABOVE The view of Via Maria from Worth Avenue. OPPOSITE Tables for a party in our via are set with Amanda Lindroth Collection lanterns and hurricanes. OVERLEAF The party scene, viewed from the stairs leading to our apartment.

ISLAND HOPPING DAYS

I have many special memories of special celebrations on verandas and terraces, and I have designed my collection of tabletop wares, furniture, and other bits and pieces with these celebrations and outdoor spaces in mind.

Since moving full time to the Bahamas in my thirties, I have been lucky enough to have been hosted and to host in many outdoor places. Weather does not daunt us when planning alfresco events, and I must confess to never having much of a rain plan. In most cases, a dash inside with plate and glass in hand can save the party when it starts to pour. I'll never forget dining on a terrace suspended over the bay at the GoldenEye resort in Jamaica when the first wave of a hurricane hit with such force that it took out the power. The dramatic sprint to our cottage was splendid!

In the late spring of 2017 I jumped on a plane to Asia armed with a dog-eared, spiral-bound notebook bulging with ideas, doodles, and inspirations I had jotted down over the years. In particular, there were sketches of items for our indoor-outdoor way of life that were missing in the marketplace and that I thought I might like to make.

On that initial trip, and a few subsequent ones, we concentrated on tabletop wares, producing basic things such as oven-proof bakeware that comes to the table in our rattan basket holders. Items like these had been available in hardware stores and supermarkets in my childhood but had disappeared and not been available for decades. We also designed accessories such as planters and wonderful overscale lanterns and hurricanes. And we hand-printed fabrics for table linens. Every step of the way, we tried to keep the collection lighthearted, full of charm, and infused with nostalgia for a simpler time.

After the great success of that first collection, we dove into furniture and added decorative items. My newest collection includes a sky-high rattan bed and whimsical wicker pagodas for table fun.

Life at Hope Hill, my family's home in the Bahamas, is centered on our veranda. All meals are served there, all celebrations happen there, and puzzles and games are played there. My collection's DNA is derived from a very happy outdoor life at Hope Hill.

OPPOSITE My vintage revival Paradise canopy bed holds court in the center of my tented Charleston shop.

ABOVE The all-rattan Brighton étagère fills this shiplap-clad entrance hall with island charm. Fresh palm fronds adorn Harbour Island lanterns when they are not being used to welcome party guests with flickering candles.
OPPOSITE A 32-inch-tall wicker pagoda decorated with bougainvillea rises amid Short Knot Bamboo and Sunburst picture frames in a multitude of sizes.

OPPOSITE Surrounded by Harbour Island lanterns, a Lyford bar table dazzles, beckoning guests to an alfresco evening. ABOVE Indoors, the Lyford bar table is styled to the nines with a sweet rectangular pagoda, cane-wrapped Hourglass hurricanes, and a pair of pink sailor's valentines. OVERLEAF Fresh green table linens, Island Wrapped glasses and votives, and, of course, pagodas create an inviting lunchtime table in Palm Beach. Take a seat on a rattan Ca'liza chair and leave all your cares behind!

ISLAND HOPPING DAYS ~ 289

It's all in the mix: Pitchers and hurricanes double as flower vases and orchid pots, candles glow in wicker pagodas, and a charming pink Jolly is embroidered on scalloped cocktail napkins. Scalloped edges also allow me to give napkins a pop of extra color.

ABOVE The Biscayne dining table is a true masterpiece of wicker weaving—a Tulip table like no other. A Ca'Liza armchair and dining chairs surround it. OVERLEAF Table linens create a coral sensation. Find your perfect combination from among more than six different patterns in three colors (coral, green, and blue), all block printed on cotton in India.

Collins the Cavalier King Charles Spaniel stares longingly at the treats displayed on a blue Peacock-patterned tablecloth. Chic Barbados Rattan thermoses keep tea and coffee piping hot.

TOP Legend has it that the original sailor's valentines were made on board ship by sailors returning to England from the West Indies. I have re-created two of the stunningly intricate designs. ABOVE Is there anything more chic than a wicker display bracket?

Whether woven into a mirror frame or curved into table legs, rattan can be seen everywhere in my furniture and accessories collections. Even the skin of this versatile tropical vine is woven by skilled artisans into caning patterns for my Hourglass hurricanes and a special diamond weave for my Antigua headboard. The Sloane side tables flanking the bed are among my favorites.

SOURCES

Accents of France
P.O. Box 573386
Tarzana, CA 91357
(323) 653-4006
accentsoffrance.com
DECORATIVE TREILLAGE AND ACCESSORIES FOR HOME AND GARDEN

Aldous Bertram
233 Royal Ponciana Plaza
Palm Beach, FL 33480
aldousbertram.com
MURALS AND WATERCOLORS

Amanda Lindroth
312B South County Road
Palm Beach, FL 33480
(561) 249-1205
amandalindroth.com
TABLETOP AND ISLAND ACCESSORIES AND FURNITURE

Andre Cooper
Nassau, Bahamas
(242) 477-3241
UPHOLSTERER

Anthony Lawrence-Belfair
32-33 47th Ave.
Long Island City, NY 11101
anthonylawrence.com
FURNITURE

Bahama Hand Prints
P.O. Box SS-19043
Ernest Street
Nassau, Bahamas
(242) 394-4111
bahamahandprints.com
FABRICS

Bamboo & Rattan
4900 South Dixie Highway
West Palm Beach, FL 33405
(561) 315-7295
vintagebamboorattan.com
ANTIQUE AND CUSTOM BAMBOO AND RATTAN FURNITURE

Beauvais Carpet
595 Madison Avenue
New York, NY 10022
(212) 688-2265
beauvaiscarpets.com
CARPETS AND RUGS

Besselink & Jones
90 Walton Street
Chelsea, London SW3 2HP, UK
+44 20 8574 4068
besselink.com
LIGHTING

Bielecky Brothers Ltd
979 Third Avenue, Suite 911
New York, NY 10022
(212) 753-2355
bieleckybrothers.com
WICKER AND RATTAN FURNITURE

Bonacina Vittorio
Via Galileo Galilei
22040 Lurago d'Erba, Italy
+39 031 696119
bonacinavittorio.it
ITALIAN WICKER FURNITURE

Bonny Byfield
Nassau, Bahamas
(242) 477-6856
bonny@coralwave.com
SIGN PAINTER

Brian Leaver
(631) 513-3967
brianleaver.com
DECORATIVE PAINTER

Bunny Williams Home
232 East 59th Street
3rd Floor
New York, NY 10022
(212) 935-5930
bunnywilliamshome.com
LIGHTING AND FURNITURE

C&C Milano
Via B. Zenale, 3
20123 Milan, Italy
+39 02 48015069
cec-milano.com
FABRICS

Charles Edwards
582 Kings Road
London SW6 2DY, UK
+44 (0) 20 7736 8490
charlesedwards.com
LIGHTING

Circa Who
531 Northwood Road
West Palm Beach, FL 33407
(561) 655-5224
circawho.com
VINTAGE FURNITURE

Coleen and Company
1201 Loma Avenue
Long Beach, CA 90804
(310) 606-2050
coleenandcompany.com
LIGHTING

Custom Furniture by Laitamaki
7400 Georgia Avenue
West Palm Beach, FL 33405
(561) 586-8556
CUSTOM UPHOLSTERY

De la Guardia Victoria Architects & Urbanists
224 Valencia Avenue
Coral Gables, FL 33134
(305) 444-6363
dlgvarchitects.com
ARCHITECTS

Elgin Marble
6005 US-1
Vero Beach, FL 32967
elginmarbleinc.com
MARBLE AND STONE

FGS Architecture & Design
381 Park Avenue South
Suite 915
New York, NY 10016
(646) 470-6528
fgs-a.com
ARCHITECTS

1st Dibs
200 Lexington Avenue, 10th Floor
New York, NY 10016
(646) 293-6633
1stdibs.com
ANTIQUES AND VINTAGE FURNITURE

F. S. Henemader Antiques
316 South County Road
Palm Beach, FL 33480
(561) 835-9237
fshenemaderantiques.com
ANTIQUES

Gracie
979 Third Avenue, Suite 1411
New York, NY 10022
(212) 924-6816
graciestudio.com
HAND-PAINTED WALLPAPER

Haleh Atabeigi
New York, NY
(917) 622-5347
halehpaint.com
DECORATIVE PAINTER

Heath & Company Lighting
3707 South Dixie Highway
West Palm Beach, FL 33405
(561) 833-0880
heathlighting.com
LAMPSHADES

Holland & Sherry
979 Third Avenue, Suite 1402
New York, NY 10022
(212) 355-6241
hollandandsherry.com
FABRICS AND WALLCOVERINGS

The Island Store
Nassau, Bahamas
(242) 377-1050
islandstorebahamas.com
HOME ACCESSORIES

Jamb
95-97 Pimlico Road
Belgravia, London SW1W 8PH, UK
+44 20 7730 2122
jamb.co.uk
FIREPLACES AND LIGHTING

John Derian
6 E. 2nd St.
New York, NY 10003
johnderian.com
ART AND ACCESSORIES

John Matouk & Co.
925 Airport Road
Fall River, MA 02720
(508) 997-3444
matouk.com
LINENS

John Robshaw
245 W. 29th St., Suite 1501
New York, NY 10001
(212) 594-6006
johnrobshaw.com
FABRICS

John Rosselli & Associates
979 Third Avenue, Suite 1800
New York, NY 10022
(212) 593-2060
johnrosselli.com
ANTIQUES, FABRICS, AND LIGHTING

J. Quintana Custom Upholstery
4302 22nd Street, Suite 115
Long Island City, NY 11101
(718) 361-0946
CUSTOM UPHOLSTERY

Joseph Wallace
755 Alton Road #2
Miami Beach, FL 33139
(305) 342-1491
DRAPERY AND UPHOLSTERY

Kassatly's
250 Worth Avenue
Palm Beach, FL 33480
(561) 655-5655
LINENS

Kenian Fine Rattan Furniture
2234 W. Great Neck Road, Suite C
Virginia Beach, VA 23451
(757) 481-0960
kenian.com
RATTAN FURNITURE

Lars Bolander
5013 South Dixie Highway
West Palm Beach, FL 33405
larsbolander.com
ANTIQUES

Lathen Ferguson
Nassau, Bahamas · (242) 436-0694
lathenferguson1@hotmail.com
UPHOLSTERER

Lee Jofa
979 Third Avenue, Suite 234
New York, NY 10022
(212) 688-0444
leejofa.com
FABRICS

Leontine Linens
3806 Magazine Street
New Orleans, LA 70115
(504) 899-7833
leontinelinens.com
LINENS

Les Indiennes
444 Warren Street
Hudson, NY 12534
lesindiennes.com
FABRICS

Leta Austin Foster
64 Via Mizner
Palm Beach, FL 33480
(561) 655-5489
letaaustinfoster.com
LINENS AND ACCESSORIES

Link Outdoor
13766 Beta Road
Dallas, TX 75244
(972) 385-7380
linkoutdoor.com
FABRIC

Lord and Vella
London, UK
+44 0207 235 2202
lordandvella.com
IMPORTING SERVICE

The Lusher Gallery
New York, NY
(917) 698-2090
Bermuda
(441) 295-5708
bermudacaribbeanart.com
ART

Mary Maguire
P.O. Box 94
Old Lyme, CT 06371
marymaguireart.com
ART

Mary Mahoney
336 Worth Avenue
Palm Beach, FL 33480
(561) 655-8288
marymahoney.com
TABLEWARE

McKinnon and Harris
1806 Summit Avenue
Richmond, VA 23230
(804) 384-2385
mckinnonandharris.com
OUTDOOR FURNITURE

Mecox Gardens
962 Lexington Avenue
New York, NY 10021
(212) 249-5301
mecoxgardens.com
FURNITURE AND ART

Meg Braff
92 Forest Avenue
Locust Valley, NY 11560
(516) 801-4939
megbraffdesigns.com
WALLCOVERINGS

Merrill, Pastor & Colgan
Architects
927 Azalea Lane, Suite B
Vero Beach, FL 32963
(772) 492-1983
merrillpastor.com
ARCHITECTS

Nassau Glass
P.O. Box SS-6398
Mackey Street
Nassau, Bahamas
(242) 393-8165
FRAMING AND GLASS

Nest Delray
817 NE 6th Avenue
Delray Beach, FL 33483
(561) 900-7181
VINTAGE FURNITURE

Newport Lamp & Shade
Company
22 Franklin Street
Newport, RI 02840
(401) 847-0228
newportlampandshade.com
LIGHTING

New Providence Art and Antiques
East Street
Nassau, Bahamas
(242) 328-7916
ART AND ANTIQUES

Nina Campbell
9 Walton Street
London SW3 2JD, UK
+ 44 (0) 20 7225 1011
ninacampbell.com
FABRICS AND WALLPAPER

Nobilis
979 Third Avenue, Suite 508
New York, NY 10022
(212) 980-1177
nobilis.fr
WALLCOVERINGS

Oomph
21 West Putnam Avenue
Greenwich, CT 06830
(203) 518-8068
oomphhome.com
FURNITURE AND LIGHTING

Palecek
AmericasMart, Suite 15-F-11
240 Peachtree Street NW
Atlanta, GA 30303
(404) 525-6333
palecek.com
FURNITURE

Palm Beach Regency
850 Old Dixie Highway
Lake Park, FL 33403
(561) 252-7381
palmbeachregency.com
VINTAGE FURNITURE

Paula Roemer Antiques
501 Belvedere Road
West Palm Beach, FL 33405
(561) 602-1250
paularoemerantiques.com
ANTIQUES AND VINTAGE
FURNITURE

Phillip Jeffries
979 Third Avenue, Suite 503
New York, NY 10022
(212) 755-6555
phillipjeffries.com
WALLCOVERINGS

Quadrille
979 Third Avenue, Suite 1415
New York, NY 10022
(212) 753-2995
quadrillefabric.com
FABRICS AND WALLCOVERINGS

The Raj Company
1-C, K. Khadye Marg
Mahalazmi, Mumbai 400 034
India
+91 (22) 2354 2626
therajcompany.com
CUSTOM CARVED FURNITURE

Robert Straub
Nassau, Bahamas · (242) 427-3042
ART INSTALLER

Samuel & Sons
983 Third Avenue
New York, NY 10022
(212) 704-8000
samuelandsons.com
TRIM

Santa Barbara Designs
201 N Rice Avenue, Suite K
Oxnard, CA 93030
(800) 919-9464
santabarbaradesigns.com
POOL UMBRELLAS

Schumacher
979 Third Avenue, Suite 832
New York, NY 10022
(212) 415-3900
fschumacher.com
FABRICS AND WALLCOVERINGS

Selamat
231 South Maple Avenue
South San Francisco, CA 94080
(650) 243-4840
selamatdesigns.com
RATTAN FURNITURE

Serena and Lily
10 Liberty Ship Way, Suite 350
Sausalito, CA 94965
(415) 331-4199
serenaandlily.com
FURNITURE AND HOME GOODS

Sika Design
(866) 910-7452
sikadesignusa.com
RATTAN FURNITURE

Soane Britain
50-52 Pimlico Road
London SW1W 8LP, UK
+44 20 7730 6400
soane.co.uk
FURNITURE AND LIGHTING

Stark Carpet
979 Third Avenue, 11th Floor
New York, NY 10022
(212) 752-9000
starkcarpet.com
CARPETS AND RUGS

Studio Four
900 Broadway, Suite 201
New York, NY 10003
(212) 475-4414
studiofournyc.com
CARPETS, RUGS, FABRICS,
AND WALLCOVERINGS

Tropical Trading
Units 1/3 40 Airport Industrial Park
Nassau, Bahamas · (242) 556-8053
tropicaltradingcompany.com
FURNITURE

Tyrone Thompson
Nassau, Bahamas · (242) 825-4251
flooritall@yahoo.com
CARPET INSTALLER

The Urban Electric Co.
2130 N. Hobson Avenue b
N. Charleston, SC 29405
(843) 723-8140
urbanelectricco.com
LIGHTING

Vanderhurd
17 Portobello Road
London W11 3DA, UK
+44 207 313 5400
vanderhurd.com
RUGS AND FABRICS

Vaughan
979 Third Avenue, Suite 1511
New York, NY 10022
(212) 319-7070
vaughandesigns.com
LIGHTING

Wellington Pinder
Nassau, Bahamas · (242) 525-8354
wellypinder@gmail.com
WALLPAPER INSTALLER

ACKNOWLEDGMENTS

I have always had a keen suspicion that my dear friend Jennifer Ash Rudick may have had something to do with the note I received from Mark and Nina Magowan inviting me for a drink one cool February night a few years ago in Palm Beach. It was on that night that Mark and Nina asked if we could work on this book together. I thank Jennifer for her suspected behind-the-scenes maneuvers, and I am eternally grateful to Mark and Nina for the great pleasure it has been to work with them on this project. Their brilliant guidance brought this book to fruition.

I am most grateful to editor Jackie Decter, who worked magic with words that were often delivered as a messy stream of reminiscences; she is genius. The book owes its fresh look to the wonderful Celia Fuller. I am also thankful to Jim Spivey for his expert oversight of the book's production. Our meetings with this Vendome family were filled with laughter and lightheartedness—a wonderful collaboration that is reflected in the happy spirit of the book.

It was a colossal moment when Chesie Breen took an interest in my work in the Bahamas over a decade ago. Chesie's support and guidance have been unswerving. She is the right balance of elegant, persuasive, and impeccably effective—I am certain that her influence in design circles will be studied in the future. She is now joined by the indomitable Ellen Niven; no designer has ever had such a dynamic duo of proper support.

Chesie brought images of Ca'Liza to Newell Turner at Hearst, resulting in the cover of *Veranda* in May 2010. Newell's constant friendship has been a dream and he, along with his wonderful team—Sophie Donelson, Clint Smith, and Whitney Robinson—has been invaluable to my career. I am also very grateful to my friends at *Coastal Living*, who were early champions of my work and continue to be so.

Shooting a book on a dozen or so islands is an operation that requires a team with energy, humor, and the ability to roll with the punches. I owe an enormous amount of gratitude to my brilliant photographer Tria Giovan, who, as an island girl herself, rolled with every punch and gave this book her A game. Tria's eye is flawless and I am so thankful to her.

I am also indebted to stylist Liz Strong. The images throughout the book are reflective of her extraordinary talent, which brought an unparalleled *joie de vivre* to these island projects. Liz's tireless energy to get just the right details in every shot had us climbing trees for coconuts and trespassing to snip the perfect bloom. Thank you, Liz!

To Aldous Bertram, whose illustrations add so much to the book, thank you. When you arrived to work with us, who knew how much fun we would all have! Your talent is boundless and you keep us laughing. What a gift.

Island Hopping is the realization of a decade of work. Designing houses on islands is a challenge and none of it would be possible without the talent of my team in both Nassau (Caro, Celine, Christina, Daniella, Denise, Erna, Joanne, Kirsten, and Sofia) and Palm Beach (Aldous, Allison, Austin, Jackie, Emily, and Tara). We spend our time loading small planes, boats, and barges, containers and golf carts with the precious items that make up the interiors of the spaces we design. This wonderful group of people has overcome every obstacle, from wild weather to containers falling overboard and everything in between. Their talent and humor make all this possible and fun. In these endeavors we rely heavily on the support of our network of architects, contractors, handymen, movers, painters, and pilots.

I am also grateful to those at home who help me create this island life on a daily basis: Amy, Eva, and Homer. So many of the parties in the book were made possible by their hard work, as well as that of chef Adrian and C.J. Our busy lives would not be possible without them.

I am very grateful to all my clients and friends who opened their doors to us. Your generosity of spirit is appreciated so much. To Gil and Tricia Besing especially, with whom I have collaborated at the Dunmore on Harbour Island for nine years now: thank you. We couldn't have imagined that this little inn tucked in the pink dune would become such an iconic place and my long-standing calling card.

Among my many dear and generous friends, I must particularly thank those who guided me on this book: Ashley Bernhard, Nina Campbell, Jackie de Ravenel, John Fondas, John Knott, Alixe Laughlin, and Tom Scheerer.

I am thankful above all for my beloved daughter, Eliza, and my brilliant husband, Orjan: you are both my sunshine.

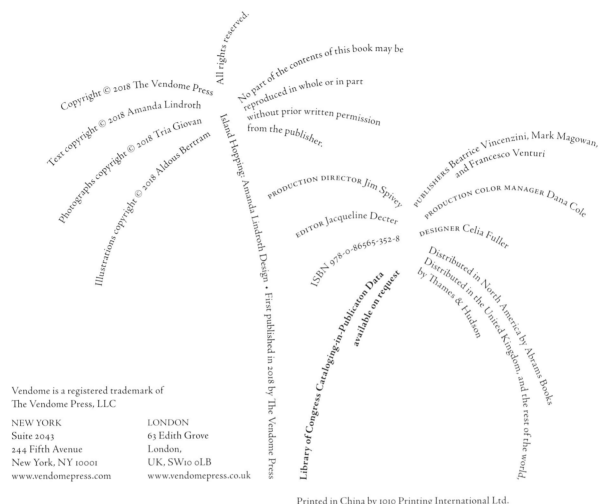

Copyright © 2018 The Vendome Press

Text copyright © 2018 Amanda Lindroth

Photographs copyright © 2018 Tria Giovan

Illustrations copyright © 2018 Aldous Bertram

All rights reserved.

No part of the contents of this book may be reproduced in whole or in part without prior written permission from the publisher.

Island Hopping: Amanda Lindroth Design • First published in 2018 by The Vendome Press

PRODUCTION DIRECTOR Jim Spivey

EDITOR Jacqueline Decter

ISBN 978-0-86565-352-8

Library of Congress Cataloging-in-Publication Data available on request

PUBLISHERS Beatrice Vincenzini, Mark Magowan, and Francesco Venturi

PRODUCTION COLOR MANAGER Dana Cole

DESIGNER Celia Fuller

Distributed in North America by Abrams Books
Distributed in the United Kingdom, and the rest of the world, by Thames & Hudson

Vendome is a registered trademark of
The Vendome Press, LLC

NEW YORK
Suite 2043
244 Fifth Avenue
New York, NY 10001
www.vendomepress.com

LONDON
63 Edith Grove
London,
UK, SW10 0LB
www.vendomepress.co.uk

Printed in China by 1010 Printing International Ltd.
Sixth printing

PHOTO CREDITS

All photographs by Tria Giovan, with the exception of the following:

Björn Wallander: pp. 16 right, 18–19, 22 top left, top right, and bottom left, 23
Annie Schlechter: pp. 4, 94–103
Brie Williams: pp. 104–11
Francesco Lagnese: pp. 112–17
Lisa Romerein: 172–81
James Merrell: pp. 206–15
Thomas Loof: pp. 256–69
Jonny Valiant: pp. 270–83
Lucy Cuneo: pp. 284–299

PAGE 2 The living room of my Palm Beach apartment on Worth Avenue. Grand green and pink chinoiserie with a dose of island accessorizing.

PAGE 4 The view from the front veranda of a fisherman's cottage at Schooner Bay, Great Abaco, is of Little Bridge Beach. Basic painted wood, Adirondack chairs, and cotton rugs are my go-to elements for these rustic out-island locations.

FRONT COVER Interior of a thatched cabana in Schooner Bay, Abaco (see also page 162).

BACK COVER In the stair hall of a house in Lyford Cay, a Victorian bamboo hat rack holds a collection of Bahamian bags and hats (see also page 74).